WOMEN IN A MEN'S CHURCH

Edited by

Virgil Elizondo
and
Norbert Greinacher

English Language Editor
Marcus Lefébure

T. & T. CLARK
Edinburgh

THE SEABURY PRESS
New York

1980
T. & T. Clark Ltd., 36 George Street, Edinburgh EH2 2LQ
ISBN: 0 567 30014 5

The Seabury Press, 815 Second Avenue, New York, N.Y. 10017
ISBN: 0 8164 2276 1

Library of Congress Catalog Card No.: 80 50478

Printed in Scotland by William Blackwood & Sons Ltd., Edinburgh

Concilium: Monthly except July and August.
Subscriptions 1980: All countries (except U.S.A. and Canada) £23·00 postage and handling included; U.S.A. and Canada $54.00 postage and handling included. (Second class postage licence pending at New York, N.Y.) Subscription distribution in U.S. by Expediters of the Printed Word Ltd., 527 Madison Avenue, Suite 1217, New York, N.Y. 10022.

CONCILIUM

Religion in the Eighties

CONCILIUM

Concilium 134 (4/1980): Practical Theology

CONTENTS

Part IV
New Beginnings

Editorial

Has Men's Liberation Gone too far?

JILL TWEEDIE, editor of the women's page of *The Guardian* (London and Manchester) received an invitation from no less distinguished a group than the Oxford Union Society to be one of the main speakers on the motion: 'That female emancipation has gone too far.' She answered the invitation in an open letter (*The Guardian*, 20th September 1979) part of which went as follows: 'There is, of course, one motion . . . that really is one of the crucial questions of the twentieth century: "That male emancipation has gone too far.". . . There are still, upon this planet, emancipated members of the male sex who designate themselves Kings, Emperors, Shah of Shahs, and Presidents in Perpetuity who claim Divine Right to torture and kill countless of their subjects in one way or another with the help of other members called the police or the military and the aid of foreign rulers in reputedly democratic or shamelessly totalitarian governments. If you want to trace the sources of starvation in the part of the world called Third, you must look to profoundly emancipated agribusinessmen who turn poor countries into battery hens to fill their own mouths and pockets. . . . Socially emancipated men are spending three million pounds per minute on arms throughout the world, intellectually emancipated men are using more than half the world's research funds on weapon research.'

These opinions are questionable and must be questioned, especially when they give rise to the impression that all misunderstandings are due exclusively to the excessive liberation of men. It nevertheless remains the case that a false distribution or fixing of roles between the sexes is an important cause of a great deal of individual and social suffering in this world and that this central problem and its manifold ramifications have not broken through to the consciousness of the public. Jill Tweedie's disturbing question about whether men's liberation has not gone too far brings out an important point which we have to consider most carefully as we work through it. Precisely because we live in a society that has been so largely shaped in a patriarchal way, the decisive, though not exclusive, question is that of changing the *man's* role. The man has to be freed from the dominating, authoritarian and blinkering role that estranges him from

vii

himself. The liberation of the oppressed must always go hand-in-hand with the liberation of the oppressors.

Against such a background, a consideration of the situation in the Church, and especially of the Catholic Church, is liable to throw one into deep gloom. Above all, we have to admire those women who go on fighting despite defamatory, deeply unchristian Church laws, doctrinal statements, Roman decrees and, above all, Church practices. But here too the same principle applies: it is men and women together who must work for a sane and more flexible pattern distribution of roles. This is why we resisted the obvious temptation of allowing only women to write in this issue. The dominance of men can be undone and the freedom of women can be achieved in society and in the Church only where men and women contribute their joint experiences and all show themselves capable of learning and changing and are prepared to redefine their roles.

Such a new definition of gender roles is also a condition of the human integration of sexuality into individual, social and Church life, and here we still have a long way to go. For the suppression of women is always tied up with a suppression of sexuality.

'Mulier tacet in Concilio?' asks one writer with complete justification. This issue could perhaps result in *Concilium* having a change of heart itself.

VIRGIL ELIZONDO
NORBERT GREINACHER

PART I

Historical Development

Ida Raming

From the Freedom of the Gospel to the Petrified 'Men's Church': The Rise and Development of Male Domination in the Church

1. INTRODUCTION

THE EXPRESSION 'Men's Church' is intended in the main to indicate the following characteristics and structural features of the Church: the holders of all ecclesiastical offices (diaconate, presbyterate and episcopate) are exclusively men; leadership and pastoral oversight are closely bound up with those offices, and the various functions connected with them (teaching, legislation and administration) are consequently exercised only by men; women have no share in them (this finds legal expression in C.I.C. 968, 1). Women can only be involved in pastoral and catechetical work in a very limited way—if at all—in certain restricted areas of the Church's life. Theological teaching and research are the domain of (clerical) men. The way in which the idea of God is expressed corresponds to the actual power structure: he is male (Father, Lord). Ecclesiastical language, as well as visual representations, confirm and sanction male predominance in the Church. They establish the full humanity of men, while making clear to women that their full humanity is questionable. Since God is portrayed as male, the assertion about being made in the image of God lacks conviction so far as women are concerned, and is left very much in the air.

3

Male dominance in the Church naturally affects all organisation, all relationships, indeed the whole of theology. Even Mariology is no exception; in fact Mary is simply there to redress the balance in a Church which, for the rest, is patriarchally oriented. She has no real significance for women, so far as their position in the Church is concerned.

In what follows, the reasons why the Church finds itself in a situation in which it can aptly be described as a Men's Church are investigated and the lines of its historical development indicated, but within this narrowly restricted framework there is room only to describe a few basic aspects and tendencies which have led to the present situation. In the main this exposition is intended to act as a reminder of what has in part already been demonstrated elsewhere in particular studies.[1]

Is such a reminder at all necessary or meaningful? It is all too easy for an institution which can look back on an existence of almost 2,000 years to be satisfied with the *status quo*, treat it as final, and solidify into immovable structures. Enquiry and research into history, a comparison of the present situation with the historical developments which have led to it, some knowledge of the reasons behind existing laws and regulations—all these help to guard against the dogmatising of what is, after all, only a historical development. To this extent we are obliged to have recourse to history. Indeed it is indispensable, if the institution is to be kept alive. This is particularly relevant to the Catholic Church. By calling itself in question as it looks in the mirror of its own history, it could save itself from setting hard and solid in this as in other questions, and it could receive a new impetus for the future.

2. THE POSITION OF WOMEN ACCORDING TO THE NEW TESTAMENT, AGAINST THE BACKGROUND OF LATE JUDAISM

In the difficult task of describing the position and status of women according to the teaching of the New Testament, it is necessary to pay attention, so far as this remains possible, to the social and cultural background of the New Testament. Only so can we guard against coming to wrong conclusions. The influence of the environment of late Judaism on the New Testament is such that without a knowledge of its social structures the New Testament teaching about women cannot be rightly evaluated or interpreted.

The description of woman as the property of the man reflects the dominant standpoint of late Judaism.[2] In consequence the woman is restricted to the house. The legal disabilities and the moral and ethical disqualifications of women correspond closely to each other: women-heathen-uncultured and women-slaves-children are placed on the same rung of the ladder.[3] Woman serves as a symbol of what is evil: that is the inference to be drawn from late classical exegesis of Genesis 3, according to which Eve is characterised as the origin of sin. In this way the anthropological and ethical dissimilarity of the sexes was given an exegetical and theological foundation. The directions for synagogue worship are purely and simply the outworking of this evaluation of women: for a service to take place, only the presence of the men was necessary; reading from the Torah or participating in the Passover was not permissible for women; and, further, they were debarred from appearing as witnesses in court. Under these conditions women could be given no official functions. Perhaps these strict standards could not be fully adhered to in the (Greek and Roman) Diaspora, since it was not unknown in Graeco-Roman society, especially in the large cities, for women to be relatively free and independent.[4]

These environmental factors (very briefly described) could not fail to have their effect upon the way women were regarded and treated during the period covered by the New Testament writings, though it must be recognised that, so far as we know from the four Gospels, the teaching and attitude of Jesus himself contrast agreeably with the rabbinical undervaluing of women. Of course this does not mean that Jesus put forward a socio-political programme for the liberation of women, or— with the probable exception of the question of divorce[5]—that he explicitly opposed rabbinical teaching about them. However, in his conduct he cultivated a free, unaffected relationship with women, marked by a respect for their person—a relationship which was free from dualistic and ascetic taboos.[6]

For the rest, no other comments of Jesus on the questions we are considering are extant. We may suppose that women belonged to the group of Jesus' disciples, but it seems unlikely that he left his followers any blueprint for the organisation and structure of his Church.[7] But even if an official appointment and sending out of the apostles could be traced back to Jesus himself, and he had called only men for this service, that would be no evidence of an explicit and deliberate act of Jesus in the sense that he wished to restrict this office to men only, as the Vatican Declaration on the question of the admission of women to the priesthood (v.J. 1976) concludes. In other words, we must draw a distinction between the attitude of Jesus to women as individuals—an attitude which is free from any kind of discrimination—and his position in relation to sociologically determined structures: the ministry as public service, an exclusively male preserve in the Jewish context, falls into sociological categories which are not susceptible to the direct reforming attempt of a single person. Therefore the fact that Jesus conformed to the existing sociological structures is not to be interpreted as an endorsement of them.

Behind such an interpretation lies a fundamental misunderstanding of the spirit of Jesus, since he left us in no doubt as to how he wished office in the Church to be understood. It was to be understood exclusively as *service* and not as an instrument of domination, which in practice it has become through the explicit, legally based, exclusion of women. It was not the intention of Jesus that any Christian leadership group should arise and establish a hierarchical relationship between itself and all other Christians, whether through the usurpation of exalted or authoritarian titles, or through the enjoyment of privileges. There is evidence for this in his disapproval of the use of the title 'Father' (Matt. 23:8-11; see also Matt. 20:25-28).[8]

In the first phase of missionary activity of the early Church, in the setting of Graeco-Roman culture, this conception of office as service, not restricted to one sex, seems to have been still effective. The need to spread the Gospel in view of Christ's imminent return was so much to the fore that any help was more than welcome. Middle-class women of some means, and probably independent, were often the first recipients of the new message, and they themselves then undertook responsibility for spreading it further (see Rom. 16:1 f.; 1 Cor. 16:19; Acts 16:14 f.), not simply in the capacity of hostesses of house fellowships but as leaders of local churches (Rom. 16:1 f.; 16:7).[9] Even the activity of female prophets was known and valued in the Pauline churches (1 Cor. 11:5; Acts 2:17). The charismatic conception of service in the Church, which allowed a profusion of different gifts to be brought into play—or, putting it negatively, the lack of a firm organisation and ministerial hierarchy—made it possible for women to take an active part in the building up, the leadership and the life of the early Christian communities.

The relatively independent and freer way of life of women in the large cities of the Graeco-Roman world provided more favourable conditions for all this than the situation of Jewish women.[10] Thus in practice Paul made use of existing conditions in the Hellenistic communities. However, it would be quite wrong to suppose that because Paul preached the equality of all before God (Gal. 3:28) he went on to deduce from it social consequences concerning the situation of women in his churches. He distinguishes only too clearly between the regime of grace in Christ, which implies the equality of all people in Christ before God but which will only find its full realisation eschatologically, and the so-called regime of creation, which finds expression in this world in the existing social structures. So far as the latter is concerned, according to Paul, the law of the subordination of woman to man applies (1 Cor. 11:3-10; Eph. 5:22-24). This is something on which Jewish tradition and Greek thought are cleverly agreed. The principle is consistently applied also in the so-called tables of household duties in the New Testament letters (Col. 3:18-4:1; Eph. 5:22-6:9; 1 Pet. 3:1-7). With the gradual waning of the expectation of Christ's imminent return, the ordering of the Pauline communities loses its charismatic character. Its place is taken by a developing and hardening formal structure modelled on the traditional patriarchal institutions of Judaism and Hellenism, and so the principle of the subordination of women, at first applied only within the family and the marriage-relationship, comes to apply also to the way the community is ordered.[11]

From this it is clear how precarious and uncertain, how far from being accepted as normal, was the service of women in the New Testament churches, by comparison with the position of men. In the deutero-Pauline Pastoral Epistles (dating from around A.D. 100), which consist mainly of rules and regulations for office-holders, and which have in view the institutionalisation and consolidating of the official hierarchy, a clear word of instruction for women is given: 1 Tim. 2:8-15. The prohibition is supported exegetically by a reference to the creation of woman after man, and to the part played by woman in the fall, according to Genesis 3—'proofs' of woman's inferiority.

Very similar in content and wording is the passage 1 Cor. 14:33-36, which is to be regarded as an interpolation, and which seeks to justify the ecclesiastical establishment of the early second century by an appeal to Paul.[12] The misogynistical elements already present in Paul—his ethical and spiritual undervaluation of women (1 Cor. 11:3 ff.; 2 Cor. 11:3)— come here to full fruition. The pieces of advice addressed to his community in a particular situation (1 Cor. 11:13-16) have, in the interim, been turned into abstract laws, which have been influenced by bourgeois ethical conceptions concerning the duties of wives and mothers.[13] It is such passages as these, and not the ones which bear witness to the active participation of women in the life of the Pauline churches, which ever since, right down to the present day, have been quoted as decisive support for the inferior status of women in the Church.[14]

In spite of these fundamental restrictions and discriminations, the Pastoral Epistles still recognise that there is a form of service in the Church for women—in the order of church widows (1 Tim 5:3-16), and in the office of deaconess (1 Tim 3:11).[15] All the different factors which have contributed to the banishment of women from participation in the official life of the Church and their relegation to a completely passive inferior role are to be clearly seen in the development of these specifically women's offices.

3. THE DEVELOPMENT OF EARLY CHRISTIAN OFFICES FOR WOMEN

So far as the order of widows is concerned, it seems that we have to do with an independent form of female presbyterate which arose because of the cultural situation of Churches in an oriental setting which required strict separation of the sexes. Hence the duties of the widow consisted of the pastoral care of women in their homes, accompanied by charitable service. In addition, the service of prayer is explicitly mentioned. The functions of the widow are already clearly restricted in the Syrian *Didascalia*, a book of Church order which dates from the first decade of the third century, and which appeals to the authority of the apostles as a defence against heretical currents. The widow is forbidden to undertake any religious instruction, even in a small group, and she is strictly excluded from the administration of the sacraments (forbidden to baptise). She is shackled to the house, and must confine herself to the service of prayer. She is thus marked out as an ascetic.

According to the sources, the progressive restriction of the rights and activities of widows in the Church is to be attributed to the strengthening of the monarchical episcopate, which the compiler of the *Didascalia* clearly supports.[16] The widow, the counterpart to the male presbyter, is seen and feared as a rival not only to the developing male diaconate, but also to the presbyteral and episcopal offices. On the same grounds—fear that the widows might claim for themselves the rights of presbyters—the Council of Laodicea (343) declares that in future women may not be appointed as elders (*presbyterae*) in the Church.[17] The old-style presbyters have in effect become cultic priests with sacramental functions, which, it is believed, must be denied to women. This brings to light a further reason for the refusal to women of official participation in the life of the Church, over and above the formation and consolidation of the clerical hierarchy: the struggle against the teaching and missionary activity of women in communities regarded as heretical.[18]

In place of the charismatically oriented order of widows, limited to prayer and perhaps still to caring for the sick, the *Didascalia* therefore institutes the female diaconate, which is intended to be a passive tool of the bishop, with a fixed place in the ecclesiastical hierarchy. Some of the functions performed by the widows are passed on to the deaconesses, though nothing is left of the former baptismal function, apart from certain subordinate duties in connection with the baptism of women by immersion (for example the anointing of the body, for reasons of decency).

So far as the office of deaconess is concerned, the development which began in the Syrian *Didascalia* reached its conclusion in a document which appeared about 100 years later, the *Apostolic Constitutions*, the most important pseudo-apostolic collection of legal and liturgical material from the fourth century. The arguments for prohibiting women from teaching and baptising show evidence of some exceedingly strong tendencies to hold women in contempt: 'If the man is the head of the woman, then it is not seemly for the rest of the body (= the woman) to rule the head. . . . That is to say, if the man is the head of the woman and he is called to the priesthood, then it is against all justice to overturn the arrangement made by the Creator and make over to the lowest limb prerogatives which have been granted to the man; for the woman is the man's body, she is made from his rib and put in subjection under him, which is also why she has been chosen to bear children.'[19].

Although the deaconess holds, through ordination, a particular place in the official ordering of the Church and is regarded as belonging to the clergy, it is nevertheless quite clear that her office is sharply distinguished from those held by men, that it is subordinate to them, and shows the effects of anti-feminism. For that reason alone, the danger of its being suppressed is ever present. As ascetic currents, themselves going back to Jewish-Christian-gnostic influences as well as to neo-platonic conceptions, made increasing inroads into the life of the Church, the original freedom in relations between the sexes (traces of which could still be found) was finally destroyed: the deaconess was drawn into the ascetic life-style of the virgin dedicated to God, she was forced back into the cloistered life and excluded from public service in the Christian community.[20]

This is the end of the official service of women in the Church, both in the East and in the West, though from another point of view a different development of this office is to be found in both regions. In the decisions of several Gallican synods of the fourth and sixth centuries, prohibiting the ordination of deaconesses, there appears yet another tendency which must not pass unnoticed. It throws light on certain anti-feminist currents which came into the Church in the wake of an increasing sacralisation of worship after the pattern of Old Testament ritual regulations. Women are excluded from cultic functions not least because of their 'monthly impurity',[21] a consequence of the revival, at the end of the classical period and in the early middle ages, of the Old Testament regulations about purity.

4. THE INFLUENCE OF THE CHURCH FATHERS ON THE PLACE AND WORTH OF WOMEN

Thus as orthodox Christianity developed more and more into an established state religion, and was obliged to resist communities which were regarded as heretical, it became explicitly anti-feminist and opposed to women's emancipation. Both the early Church theologians and the Church Fathers of the fourth to sixth centuries played an important part in this development. Influenced by the conception of the anthropological and ethical inferiority of women, they confine them to two possible life styles: either they can be wives and mothers, who as faithful matrons are strictly excluded from public affairs and submit obediently to their hus-

B

bands, or they can choose virginity, in which case they must rise above their feminity, which is the embodiment of hostility to God, of moral danger and of weakness, and so become spiritually men.[22] This was the answer the Fathers gave to the question of women as it presented itself in their day. They found ideological support for it on the one hand in Roman law, which because of its conservative morality was already considerably divorced from reality, and on the other in biblical passages (Gen. 3:6; 6:2) which seemed to them to confirm their conception of woman as the source of sin and the seducer of man.

5. THE REPRESSION OF WOMEN BY THE THEOLOGY AND CANON LAW OF THE MIDDLE AGES

Patristic views on the worth of women continue to exert a determinative spiritual influence also on the period which follows. The authority of the Church Fathers was held in such high esteem in the middle ages that their pronouncements were regarded as virtually infallible, comparable to the decisions of Councils and ordinances of the pope. Especially in the field of the exposition of Scripture, the Fathers were indisputably accorded pre-eminence. In his *Book of Decrees* (written about 1140) Gratian makes use of their exegesis of the Pauline and deutero-Pauline passages to which we have referred in order to establish and justify the 'position of slavish subjugation' which he assigns to women— subjugation which requires them 'to be subject to men in everything (*dictum* p. c.11, C.33 q.5).[24] In this period, the exclusion of women from the official area of the Church's life is more and more taking on juridical forms. Thus the *Decretum Gratiani* offers to women only prohibitions, which deny to them the exercise of pastoral functions as well as cultic or liturgical participation.

Since the *Decretum Gratiani* superseded all older collections of laws right up to the end of the twelfth century, and, though it was the work of a private individual, was officially recognised by Gregory XIII as the first part of the *Corpus Iuris Canonici*, its influence on the period which followed can hardly be overestimated. Thus the *Decretals* of Gregory IX (1234) supplement the regulations for women already contained in the *Decretum* of Gratian with even wider prohibitions (on preaching, on hearing confession, on serving at the altar). Various factors to which we have already referred combine to provide the motive behind these prohibitions: the complete sacralisation of worship after the pattern of the Old Testament; related to that, the Old Testament regulations about ritual purity; ascetic tendencies (the regulation about celibacy for priests); above all the conception of the anthropological and ethical inferiority of women and their consequent *status subiectionis*, all supported by the authority of the Bible, the Church Fathers and Roman law. In the theological and canonistic literature of the Middle Ages a complete argument is developed to prove the unfitness of women for ordination: the '*constitutio ecclesiae facta propter sexum*', that is the considered opinion of the Church concerning the female sex, is against the ordination of women.[25] Discrimination against the female sex is here clearly stated in plain language, as in the arguments of Thomas Aquinas.[26] All these arguments show the causal relationship which exists between the disparagement of women and their position in the Church. This relationship is also determinative for the doctrine built on it and the laws relating to it—just as it was for the theology of the middle ages and the relevant regulations of the *Corpus Iuris Canonici*.

6. CONTINUING ANTI-FEMINISM IN THE CATHOLIC CHURCH OF TODAY

The patriarchal basis of the Church with all its implications was confirmed afresh by the publication in 1976 of the Declaration of the Congregation for the Doctrine of the Faith on the question of the admission of women to the priesthood. The key sentence of the Declaration: 'The Church, in fidelity to the example of the Lord, does not consider herself authorised to admit women to priestly ordination'[27] reveals the unsympathetic spirit which pervades the document and is its characteristic mark. Lacking the necessary reverence for the spirit and person of Jesus, and apparently not prepared to undertake honest historical analysis or to take account of the results of research already undertaken, the compilers of the document project their patriarchal attitude on to Jesus in order to sanction male dominance with divine authority.[28]

The untenability of the position taken by the Declaration is further to be seen in the following: Whereas in the theology of the early Church and the Middle Ages the status of women is linked with their supposed inferiority, according to the Declaration their status must be seen as an expression of the otherness, the differentiation of women from men.[29] Nothing can blind those who think critically, those who have learnt from the history of theology and the Church, to the fact that in the last resort all such reasoning is based on the premise of the inferiority of women and their resultant subordinate status. This applies both to the symbolic argument which falls into this category (that the priest represents Christ, the man represents the head of the Church, the woman the Church as the Bride of Christ—whence spring their 'different' functions in the Church), and to the similar reasoning which underlies the newer technology and the Declaration.

In view of this reaction on the part of the responsible authorities, in view of their intransigence in face of the fully justified efforts to achieve reform in the matter of women's rights, is it any wonder that a profound estrangement should be developing between women who are aware of the reasons behind their position in the Church on the one hand, and the official Church on the other? Catholic women and all reasonable people are being provoked, by the violation of the human dignity and human rights of women from the side of the patriarchal institutional Church, into developing strategies to change their situation. It is imperative that the position of women in the Church, and above all patriarchally oriented theology, should be subjected to a thorough-going revision, on the grounds that traditional theology in all its aspects serves as the principal support for the patriarchal institutional Church. In other words, the setting up and development of 'women studies' in relation to religion and the Church, together with a process of enlightenment, are an urgent necessity at the present time.[30]

Translated by G. S. S. Knowles

Notes

1. In the following arguments I am basing myself, among others, on K. Thraede, Art. 'Frau' in the *Reallexicon für Antike und Christentum VIII* (1970) pp. 197-269; *id*. 'Aerges mit der Freiheit. Die Bedeutung von Frauen in Theorie und Praxis der alten Kirche: "Freunde in Christus werden . . ."' in *Kennzeichen* I, edited by G. Schaffenorth and K. Thraede (Gelnhausen 1977) pp. 31-182; O. Bangerter *Frauen im Aufbruch. Die Geschichte einer Frauenbewegung in der Alten Kirche* (Neukirchen 1971); H. Cancik *Die neutestamentlichen Aussagen über Geschlecht, Ehe, Frau: zun Thema Frau in Kirche und Gesellschaft* (Stuttgart 1972) pp. 9-47; R. Radford Reuther 'Die Abschirmung des Allerheiligsten. Sexismus und geistliches Amt' *Wege zum Menschen* 31 (1979) 53-68.
2. This view is already present in classical Judaism: see Thraede 'Aerger . . .' p. 89.
3. See Thraede 'Aerger . . .' 88.
4. So Thraede 'Aerger . . .' 92.
5. See Cancik '*Die neutestamentichen Aussagen* . . .' p. 19.
6. Cancik *op. cit.* 20 ff.; Radford Ruether 'Die Abschirmung . . .' p. 55 f.
7. See E. Schüssler Fiorenza 'Die Rolle der Frau in der urchristlichen Bewegung' in *Concilium 12* (1976) 7.
8. See also Radford Ruether 'Die Abschirmung . . .' 56 f.
9. See Thraede 'Aerger . . .' 99.
10. See Thraede *op. cit.* 101 f.
11. See Thraede *op. cit.* 125.
12. See H. Lietzmann—W. G. Kümmel *An die Korinther I/II* (Tübingen 1949) p. 75; Thraede 'Aerger . . .' 111 f.
13. So Cancik '*Die neutestamentliche Aussagen* . . .' p. 17.
14. Paul VI, e.g., in his sermon on the occasion of the recognition of St Theresa as a teacher of the Church quotes 1 Cor. 14:34 to justify the exclusion of women

from the 'hierarchical functions of the teaching and priestly office' [*AAS* 62 (1962) 593].

15. On the relation of the two offices to each other, various hypotheses have been put forward in the course of research; see O. Bangerter *op. cit.* pp. 63 f.

16. Cf. H. Achelis—J. Fleming *Die syrische Didaskalia* (Leipzig 1904) pp. 276, 280 f.

17. So Bangerter *Frauen im Aufbruch* p. 79.

18. Cf. Bangerter *op. cit.* p. 75; Thraede 'Aerger . . .' 135.

19. *Didascalia et Constitutiones Apostolorum*, ed. F. X. Funk (Paderborn 1905) I pp. 191, 199, 201; *Apostolische Konstitutionen* (Bibliothek der Kirchenväter 63, 1874) pp. 115 f., 120.

20. See L. Zscharnack *Der Dienst der Frau in den ersten Jahrhunderten der christlichen Kirche* (Göttingen 1902) pp. 153 f., 156; Bangerter *Frauen im Aufbruch . . .* p. 121.

21. For more detailed treatment and consideration of the source-documents, see I. Raming *Der Ausschluss der Frau vom priesterlichen Amt. Gottgewollte Tradition oder Diskriminierung?* (Cologne 1973) p. 38A. 163; 39A. 168.

22. See Thraede Art. 'Frau' VIII 245.

23. So Thraede *ibid.* VIII 246.

24. On the importance of the Church Fathers in the *Decretum Gratiani* see I. Raming *Der Ausschluss . . .* pp. 54-62.

25. See Raming *ibid.* p. 163.

26. See suppl. q.39 a.1: '. . . quia, cum sacramentum sit signum, in his quae in sacramento aguntur requiritur non solum res, sed signum rei. . . . Cum igitur in sexu foemineo non possit significari aliqua eminentia gradus, quia mulier statum subiectionis habet; ideo non potest ordinis sacramentum suscipere' (*Summa Theologiae*, ed. P. Caramello (Turin/Rome 1948) IV, p. 773). The glossa ordinaria on the *Decretals* by Bernhard v. Botone (composed in 1245) says that woman cannot aspire to the spiritual power of the keys because she is not made in the image of God, and must always serve man in complete submission. See Raming *Der Auschluss . . .* pp. 140 ff. with A. 80, 81.

27. *Declaration (Inter insigniores) on the Question of the Admission of Women to the Ministerial Priesthood* (London C.T.S. 1976) Introduction.

28. What is more, it has been disclosed that it was as a result of pressure from Vatican circles that the Anglican Church in England decided against the ordination of women. Thus ecumenism is pursued at women's expense.

29. 'Equality is in no way identity, for the Church is a differentiated body, in which each individual has his or her role' (*Declaration on the Question of the Admission of Women to the Ministerial Priesthood*, § 6).

30. At the University of Nijmegen, as is well known, a project called 'Feminism and Christianity' is being run, under the leadership of Dr Mrs C. Halkes. In addition, in the Department of Catholic Theology in the University of Münster (Seminar for Religious Studies) a research project has begun with the title: 'Women in Islam and in Islamic Society' (study leader: Dr Mrs Iris Müller). This project must necessarily be extended to include the great religions most closely related to Islam (Judaism and Christianity), in order to make comparative study possible.

Ferdinand Menne

Catholic Sexual Ethics
and Gender Roles
in the Church

1. INTRODUCTION

WHY WAS this article not written by a woman? There is no satisfactory
answer to this necessary question which became all the more imperative
in the course of writing—*Mulier tacet in Concilio* (with a few significant
exceptions).

So much has been said and so much remains to be said on the present
topic that the area for discussion has to be narrowed down. As the title
indicates, this article is concerned for the most part with Catholic sexual
ethics, though there is some reference to Christian sexual ethics in general. The 'Church' is the Church in the Federal Republic of Germany, a
church which has adapted itself without friction to a late-capitalist transition society. The Church in Latin America, for example, which is in a
quite different situation, has problems of sexual ethics and politics and
solutions to them which go beyond those specific to West Germany.

To whom is this essay addressed? Certainly not to that majority of
women and men who find it bizarre or ridiculous still to expect anything
from the Church in sex matters, whether positive recommendations or
pastoral advice. Since I am principally concerned with women who are
still affected by men within the Church, my remarks are intended above
all for Church-men. I wish to offer some fraternal support for the existential, cultural and social transformation of the context in which certain
groups of women have to live:

1. Those whose work and life are within or closely connected with the Church (those employed in Church institutions, women lay-theologians, priests' housekeepers, members of religious orders).
2. Women who have abandoned some formal connection with the Church and those whose husbands have left the priesthood (the wives of 'laicised' priests).
3. Women whose religious life is lived within a Church context.

I am also to some extent concerned with the lives of those who do not think of themselves as Church-people, but who are affected by the Church's public activity (legislation, publicity campaigns, and so on).

2. CRITICAL ACCOUNT OF CHURCH HISTORY

Anyone who at present suffers under the Church's sexual ethics and the gender roles prescribed by the Church is understandably inclined to interpret Church history as a history of injustice and repression. Any such judgment nevertheless ascribes to the Church—in modern times at least—more social and cultural influence than it actually deserves. Much more service will be done to the interests of persons now living, and to attempted change, by a precise summary account of history than by a tactically appropriate selection of historical material. To that end I am content to quote Michel Foucault when he says that we should no longer be concerned merely to alter the 'entire known mechanism of repression' yet again, to produce yet another variation of its ecclesiastical instance, but to illuminate the whole pattern of power.[1]

Let me not be misunderstood. There should be no disguising of the additional repression carried out by the Church; its methods have been dark and cruel. Max Scheler once remarked justifiably, if with unscholarly anger, that the sexual morality of the Church was 'an ancient and erroneous priestly morality which sought to reduce sexual love as far as possible to the level of a mere drive and a libidinous pursuit of pleasure: partly out of that professional resentment that devalues what one must oneself forgo; partly out of fear of a possible disturbance of the mere business of reproduction (which is numerically important to the priests in a special way for the sake of the power and growth of their Church); and partly for the sake of a more noble and more profound motive, that is, in order to prevent a *contest* between divine and sexual love—which is assuredly a noteworthy danger of the highest forms of sexual love'.[2] Moreover a rhapsodist of Eros like Walter Schubart rather summarily conflates historical facts when he declares emotively and rhetorically: 'Asceticism destroys not sex but Eros. It cannot kill sex. Hence the history of asceticism is a history of dying eroticism and at the same time an index

of smouldering desires. One has only to think of the sultry atmosphere
laden with sexual tension that envelops certain confessionals. And there
are the cramped consciences of priests groaning under the burden of
celibacy. . . . How much untold suffering this one ascetic institution has
meant for the Catholic clergy throughout so many centuries—so much so
that the history of enforced celibacy may be justifiably accounted one of
the darkest aspects of the story of Christianity. Think of the theological
speculation about the *sigillum virginitatis*, and the lascivious depiction of
anatomical details which covers the mystery of the supernatural birth of
God—a field of concepts on which the overheated imagination of the
unmarried could play without restraint. And above all we have moral
theology and pastoral medicine, which often delight in the most extreme
perversions under the guise of scientific gravity'.[3]

The opinions of the Fathers who decided the doctrine of the Church are
well-known:[4] 'You have given the devil entry' (Tertullian). A fundamental influence was that of the man who was to become St Augustine.
Without ascribing a modern mentality to him, it is nevertheless clear that
he faced the erotico-sexual problems of his youth with the aid of Stoic,
Gnostic and Manichaeian pronouncements in which woman is seen as a
less valuable, de-souled apparatus of reproduction, but reproduction
itself appears as a justification of male condescension towards female
flesh. In the area of sexual ethics Augustine was even more influential
than Aquinas who had learnt from the 'philosopher' (Aristotle) that
woman was an inadequate version of man. He explained the devaluation
and subjection of woman as results of sin, and that sin had made woman
lacking, an accident as it were. We should also remember that Luther
strongly condemned celibate thinking and living but ultimately could not
free himself from their influence: 'We are all fornicators', and therefore
women may 'happily whelp until they die; after all that's what they're
there for'.[5] This is the familiar tone of men for whom female sexuality is
essentially sinister and thus to be considered only as a phenomenon to be
constrained.

These ideas are supported by the theological understanding of 'nature'.
What appears to be a biological fact is formulated as a norm and
institutionalised. Or, rather, what is socially and culturally demanded of
women is said to be their 'naturally' ordained essence.

Of course this might well have remained mere doctrine, the grey
theorising of monks working off their repressions. We have to ask what
this theory really meant and what form it actually took in the minds of
priests in the fifteenth, eighteenth and twentieth centuries, in France,
England and a retarded Germany; and what it meant for the life of a
peasant woman in Brittany, Sicily or the Black Forest of the seventeenth
or nineteenth century. It is no longer enough to follow a particular

interest and select negative or positive citations from 'Scripture and tradition' which have to bear the burden of responsibility for the male worldliness, misogynist cast or humanity of Christianity. We also have to discover what effect the traditional notions had in everyday life; how they developed and were implemented socially in mind and emotions according to the country, status, class, education and property of different individuals.

One decisive factor in the establishment of the ecclesiastical gender roles which were the everyday expression of the teachings of sexual ethics is the reservation to men (especially clergy) of the roles of power and influence. In the most favourable case women appear as 'the most favourable audience' (Goethe). On the other hand, laity-roles were moulded by the 'alliance-system' (Foucault): a system of marriage, the establishment and development of relationships, and the transmission of names and goods, which was ordered in a wholly 'patrilineal' manner and orientated to the father. Here women appear as a kind of 'walking ovary': 'Woman as a whole is the child-bearer' (Virchow).[6]

Therefore we have to investigate a 'forgotten' history—the history of the everyday life of the sexes subject to the claims of the Church. Extremely valuable insights are to be won from the concern with those approaches to the histories of love, death, mercy, cruelty, joy and fear which Lucien Febvre asked for in 1941 in the *Annales d'histoire sociale*.[7] Moreover, with a form of historical studies that sees itself as social science and a social science conscious of its historical duty, we would have to make the necessary connections with the history of the forces and conditions of production.

In feminist studies (that is, a field of research with a specific interest) there are initial approaches to the writing of an alternative form of history which have to do with the present topic, for instance investigations of the 'witches of the modern era' as the obverse of Western rational civilisation.[8]

But here I can only refer to a project which I cannot describe in even approximate terms. Therefore I shall address myself to the question of the present relationship between ecclesiastical sexual ethics and gender roles in the Church. I shall cite two examples which seem highly appropriate: the discussion about contraception and abortion, and the relation between priests and women.

3. FEMALE CASE HISTORIES AND CLERICAL DOMINATION

In 1962 Marcelle Auclair published her *Le Livre noir de l'avortement*, a collection of biographical letters from desperate women who had had abortions. At that time she believed that it was '. . . a concern of the

Church and of priests naturally and openly to answer the appeals of the faithful in the crises of conscience produced by modern life. Their task is twofold: to teach and to be merciful'.[9]

In the recent women's movement the questions of contraception and especially of abortion have become central points of confrontation. In the dispute over the reform of Article 218 (on abortion) in the Federal German legal code the Church put decisive pressure on the legislators, so that they would embody ecclesiastical moral notions in State law and punish any infringement with State power. This occurred in spite of the simultaneous insistence on condemning effective methods of birth control. The fact that the Church cannot be concerned only with the absolute protection of life is shown by its attitude to life after the womb.

This article offers insufficient space to discuss the question of abortion responsibly. I shall only repeat in regard to the Church's attitude what Karl Barth says in his *Church Dogmatics*: In comparison with the conflict between the mother's life and that of the child the Church's attitude— 'which is never lacking in extreme demands on women'—in this respect seems 'almost gruesomely respectable'.[10] Whether the Church's attitude is more gruesome or more respectable is something that ultimately only the conscience of real women can decide.

In Church sexual ethics women are verbally allowed the right to make free decisions of conscience, but then their decision and autonomy of conscience are subordinated to the 'inalienable right of the unborn child to life'. The interpretation of this right is assigned to the magisterium of the Church, and sanctions against infringements are accorded to the State courts.

Instead of showing (and drawing corresponding conclusions) how far modern, male-dominated technological thought undermines traditions, cuts off the potential of life and destroys life, an attempt is made to personalise the problem as a private question for women. Yet the logic of official Church pronouncements is tantamount to a qualification of women as deprived of conscience and responsibility.

What popes and bishops fear—namely, that humankind might try to extend through its entire history the pursuit of progress by manipulating natural forces and by their rational evaluation—has already happened.[11] There can be no return to the 'old nature' which seemed to be self-declarative. Sexual ethics and gender roles and in them the protection of life can be found and ensured only in talk about and social struggle for conscious nature, *natura nova*.[12]

Edward Shorter, a leading proponent of family studies, believes that no topic of intimate life is less accessible to investigation than married sexuality.[13] I can agree only conditionally. Even less accessible is the erotico-sexual life of 'spiritual' men and women—nuns and priests and so on. Of course there have been attempts to remove some veils. Much human suffering has been revealed. Female suffering above all, for even though there are instances of male unhappiness in this regard, men nevertheless still have greater possibilities at their disposal. There are various forms of female misery in this area, and they are evident in a variety of gender roles in the Church. I shall name a few of them. Wishes can be repressed and disappear only to recur as compulsions: for instance, the housekeeper who cares totally for, and neurotically tidies and dusts and polishes for, a man reduced to the condition of a child. Needs can be expressed as enforced sublimation: for instance, the spinster who glorifies and devotes herself to the priest-man beloved while 'forgoing' all other interests. There is the experience of impermissible pleasure and sub-sequent guilt: for instance, the priest's girl friend who cannot take it any more and seeks refuge in mental illness.

Yet this complex of problems is still successfully repressed at the collective level, with considerable success. There are various reasons for this. Many of those affected try to make their lives 'respectable' again by seeking laicisation. What does this mean? To be allowed by the official Church to follow a less worthy path because 'one just could not take it'. Whoever follows that road has in my experience to suffer resentment, anger and contempt, but seldom has the qualities demanded of the martyr that he would become if he were to publish his experiences.

For martyrdom is what happens to those who try to make public the suffering they have experienced and the suffering they are aware of. It is easy for Church-men to focus suspicion on them, to characterise them as trouble-makers, self-important, or just pathological. This sort of con-demnation is all the more successful because even those who are critical of compulsory celibacy say: 'He just couldn't take it!' But that kind of cynicism and unqualified comment helps no one.

Another reason for the conspiracy of silence is the silence of those who 'reach an arrangement', who carve out an appropriate way of life for themselves without any noise or trouble. Those bonds which hold priests and their women to erotico-sexual relationships are among the strongest that exist. They have to suffer much loneliness, secrecy, restricted inti-macy and a certain degree of innuendo. These priests—these men—rely on the discretion and courage of their women.

The fact that in this regard the Church does not broadcast its pre-servations of a secret knowledge on the part of authorities and superiors, and that behind the scenes it offers very practical but also mendacious recommendations for intimacy with women and for the sexual behaviour of Church-women, is something that essentially devalues its justification and authority. This kind of pragmatism certainly relies on the 'experience of centuries' but it is also something that will not last for centuries.

To be sure, such procedures have plausible reasons: the surrender of compulsory celibacy would weaken Catholicism as a 'political entity' and further reduce its surviving power. It is logical that a 'Holy Father' celebrated by the media as a 'manly pope' should block the laicisation of priests.

4. ATTEMPTS AT WOMEN'S LIBERATION IN THE CHURCH: ORDINATION AND FEMINIST THEOLOGY

The women's movement has also had effects in the major Christian churches.[14] An old theme—the official ordination of women—has been brought up to date. A comparison of the study of *The Question of the Ordination of Women* issued by the World Council of Churches with the declaration of the Congregation for the Doctrine of the Faith on the admission of women to the priesthood reveals the expected denominational differences. The Catholic finding is unambiguous: 'The Church, in fidelity to the example of the Lord, does not consider herself authorised to admit women to the priestly ordination.'[15]

Hans Urs von Balthasar invokes C. S. Lewis in revealing the background to this decision: 'Certainly the absolute Fatherhood of God the Father, and his representation by the Son, and the Son's representation by the man is "something which is unreasonable to the heathen and supra-reasonable to the faithful". But these things must exist in the Church if it is to remain the religion of revelation. "If we surrender the impenetrable element and affirm only that which we can justify with cunning and appropriateness before the court of enlightened reason, then we exchange revelation for an ancient magical nature-religion", with its many priestesses.'[16]

Women in the Catholic Church fight against this monopolisation of the priestly role by men. They are supported by theologians who explain the situation as traditional but not as fixed dogma.

This tendency, which we might call an attempt at equal rights by means of a clericalisation of women, has certain features in common with the general attempt to emancipate women by vocational means. On the one hand, this means assuming the same alienation as men; on the other hand, vocation (social independence, extension of personal experience, and so on) is a necessary though inadequate condition of the possibility of continuing liberation.

We have to ask whether the 'clericalisation' of women has at least this ambivalence of female work. Even if the official Church were to permit certain forms of clerical work for women, then we may rest assured that they would be extended only to particularly conformist Church-women (*virgines probatae*). We may hope that if women were ordained the

Church would not stay the same; it seems to me more probable that the women would not alter the Church system but that the male Church could change the women.

Moreover the suffering of priests in the exercise of their eroticism and sexuality would be doubled. 'Being a eunuch for the sake of the kingdom of heaven'—how often and for how long does it prove successful in a humanly mature and experientially rich way? How often is it the beginning of a private history of suffering, a history of defence-mechanisms and substitute satisfactions, of religiously coloured masochism? Pope Joan—whatever her historical status—must surely remain a phantom or a unique case.[17]

In addition to the attempt to produce a change in Church gender roles on the organisational level, another attempt is evident in regard to the ecclesio-theoretical form of knowledge which we know as theology. Above all in the United States there have been attempts at a feminist theology some of which are more intent upon reform within the Church whereas others are set on radical criticism. The decidedly critical approaches are 'post-Christian' in their implications, holding the Christian churches to be so unchangeably permeated by male domination, that women have no meaningful part to play in them. Protestant women theologians, on the other hand, speak of repressed aspects of Christianity in accordance with which man and woman are 'one in Christ'.

Some—not uncontested—aspects of this kind of feminist theology are: female religious experience; the death of God as the death of the great patriarch and of a phallocratic value system; the symbolism of man/womanhood or woman/manhood (androgyny/gynandry); an 'other' non-desexualised Mary as a symbol of female experience; non-sexist talk about God; and sisterliness/sisterhood as a critical category. Many themes of the 'secular' debate in the women's movement have been reformulated in religious terms.

This 'other' religious talk is always in danger of becoming a mere superstructure: the heart of a heartless world; the spirit of spiritless circumstances; imaginary flowers on the chains. The relation between theology and Church practice should never be excluded from consideration. In addition to the question of the form of knowledge there is that of the mode of organisation: a history of Jesus in which he does not come into the world by means of a virgin birth (in which idol, according to Schubart, there is a mixture of need for the miraculous and fear of sex), but is born of the young Jewish girl Maria/Miriam, would satisfy many people—but surely not the Congregation for the Doctrine of the Faith? What good—in the opinion of the College of Cardinals—does it do to present Jesus as a sensitive, 'real' man with a gift of understanding women? Are the 'post-Christian' feminists and Hans Urs von Balthasar right in claiming that the Catholic-Christian is so essentially male in tenor that every trace of 'another' form of knowledge appears predecided as the gathering of crumbs from the rich man's table, and incapable anyway of grounding any different practice?

A preliminary thesis shows that the sexual ethics of the Catholic Church, the Catholic model of sexual roles, give no indication of where in a reasonable time women might be able to win a place in the structures of knowledge and organisation that would be appropriate to their fight for liberation. The everyday structures of the Church can only be altered within the process of change in the general structures.

5. CONJECTURES ABOUT A DIFFERENT EVERYDAY LIFE OF THE SEXES

What perspectives are we offered in regard to critical questions about the ordination of women and the development of a feminist theology? Here the future of the sexual ethics of the Church and its consequences for the exercise of gender roles in the Church are generally in question.

The great period of ecclesiastical sexual ethics began with the penitential practices and the ascetical and mystical methods of the Middle Ages. It ended in the eighteenth century when a new 'technology of the flesh' came into being 'which was not yet free of the theme of sin, but in all essentials was outside the Church area'. The disposition of the sexes was such that education, medicine and economy turned sex into a lay and state affair, 'a matter in which the entire body of society and almost all its individuals had to withdraw from supervision'.[18]

The magisterium did not make the transition from 'alliance' to 'sexuality' but still considers the conditions of reproduction to be the normative power of biological nature and legal marriage conditions—which are particularly oppressive to women.

Refusal of the sexuality model could be productive if it were directed in argument against the new domination of the body by its medicalisation, economisation and educationalisation. But the Church rejection is directed against a new form of domination in the name of an old; therefore it cannot appear as an anti-human and therefore especially anti-feminist form of obsolescence but as sheer non-simultaneity.

Fewer and fewer women who become aware of their situation and their prospects think of themselves as an audience for this claim. Women reject the alien ecclesiastical determination of sexual ethics and gender roles; they decide for self-discovery, self-understanding and self-organisation. Women's groups offer an insulating atmosphere which gives the security to fire questions at the male Church.

Surely an affected woman who has become aware of her experience in life-historical terms can say something more decisive about protecting the life of the embryo in the mother's womb that an ancient cardinal who does not hesitate to compare abortion with the extermination of the Jews. Can a young mother who compares her own case with the biographies of other women not speak out of self-awareness with a theologian, and discuss the subject of norms which the theologian obtains as written wisdom from his colleagues—all male? Surely the plea of an erotically satisfied woman for occasional abstention would receive more consideration than the call to asceticism made by a confessor who does not know the 'melancholy of fulfilment' (Ernst Bloch)? Surely pronouncements against the 'normative power of the factual' in a late-capitalist society are more effective from the lips of a woman who actually experiences the contradiction between the plaint over a population recession and simultaneous enmity to children in everyday life?

Can an advantage in experience be compensated by a lead in theorising? Would women, if they were as unburdened and prosperous as an established German professor of theology, have less 'penetration' of problems of sexual ethics than he?

The growing courage to be self-aware about erotic knowledge, consciousness and practice, which includes in addition to needs and experience the critical memory of tradition, is not something that can be lived in isolation. It is part of an inclusive courage to lead an authentic life in which forms of alienation (and not bonds of affection) are cancelled. What an authentic women's life will look like is something that is being worked out by experiment. There is no recipe and no model that have been worked out in detail.

The opinion that particularly the women's question in the Church has to be referred to general social conditions, should not cause us to deny the necessity for measures that mediate between them. So long as women are enlightened about their conscious or unconscious dependence on Church-men, there must be a struggle within the Church for the human rights of women. In this process a feminist theology and a feminist sexual ethics will probably have a part to play. They are already using another language which shatters the axioms of the usual ecclesiastical formulas.[19]

Ultimately, however, it is not a question of a 'women's culture' as an autonomous and therefore asocial work of art. The battle about ecclesiastical sexual ethics and their consequences for gender roles in the Church is only one aspect of a greater *social* confrontation, to which it is objectively linked and must be subjectively linked if women are to become subjects of their socially-determined history.

The development of something societally new occurs in the form of contradictions. Men speak of the synthesis of the patriarchal and the matriarchal principles: motherly love through justice and reason, fatherly authority through mercy and equality (Erich Fromm). Or they talk—

going further—of the regulative idea of an androgynous society in which men like women are other than they are now, and sensitivity, receptivity and sensuousness are creatively liberating qualities for both—from the emancipation of women to emancipation of man to the emancipation of society as a whole (Herbert Marcuse).[20]

Even those men who are concerned for empathy and change encounter women who retort that man discovered the beauty of traditional female qualities when women began to develop other, less comfortable qualities; the misfortune of man and his unilateral form of life has been a subject for complaint since women began to fight aggressively for equal rights.[21]

Somewhat precipately perhaps, I should like to endorse a statement of Marcuse's: 'The problem of equal rights does not obviously force the women's movement to slow down or to surrender the struggle for equal rights. But clearly there is something beyond equal rights. And if this "beyond" is not included from the start in the struggle for equal rights, remaining a virulent part of it, then something is evidently wrong.'[22]

This 'beyond' the late-capitalist society of exploitation, competition, repression and growth is described in terms traditionally ascribed to the feminine: need-oriented, receptive, tender and caring. 'Perhaps the true society is weary of development and exercises its freedom to leave certain possibilities untouched, instead of madly striving towards alien planets.'[23] Ideas of true social life retain the knowledge that it can allow no manifestation of a false physical life and false gender roles.

Translated by J. G. Cumming

Notes

1. See M. Foucault *Histoire de la sexualité* I: *La Volonté de savoir* (Paris 1975).
2. See F. W. Menne *Kirchliche Sexualethik gegen gesellschaftliche Realität* (Munich 1971) p. 231.
3. W. Schubart *Religion und Eros* (Munich 1966) p. 252.
4. See M. Müller *Grundlagen der katholischen Sexualethik* (Regensburg 1968); D. Savramis *Des sogenannte schwache Geschlecht* (Munich 1972).
5. See J. Burri *'Als Mann und Frau schufer sie': Differenz der Geschlechter aus moral- und praktisch-theologischer Sicht* (Zürich 1977).

6. See Müller *Grundlagen* cited in note 4, p. 69.

7. See L. Febvre 'La Sensibilité et l'histoire. Comment reconstituer la vie affective d'autrefois?' in *Annales d'histoire sociale* No. 3 (1941) 5-20. See also: J.-L. Flandrin *Familles* (Paris 1976); D. Kamper & V. Rittner (eds.) *Zur Geschichte des Körpers. Perspektiven der Anthropologie* (Munich 1976); J. van Ussel *Sexualunter-drückung. Geschichte der Sexualfeindschaft* (Reinbek bei Hamburg 1970).

8. See C. Honegger (ed.) *Die Hexen der Neuzeit. Studien zur Sozialgeschichte eines kulturellen Deuteungsmusters* (Frankfurt 1978) (includes an extensive international bibliography). See also: H. P. Duerr *Über die Grenze zwischen Wildnis und Zivilisation* (Frankfurt ²1978).

9. M. Auclair *Das tödliche Schweigen. Eine Umfrage über die Abtreibung* (Olten 1964) p. 126.

10. See Menne *Sexualethik* edited in note 2, at p. 83.

11. See Menne *ibid.* p. 213. On the evolution of a general concept of nature and reason, see C. Urban *Nominalismus im Naturrecht. Zur historischen Dialektik des Freiheitsverständnisses in der Theologie* (Düsseldorf 1979).

12. See D. Claessens *Nova Natura. Anthropologische Grundlagen modernen Denkens* (Düsseldorf 1970).

13. See E. Shorter *The Making of the Modern Family* (New York and London 1975).

14. An excellent survey (with an account of the literature up to 1978) is to be found in: H. Meyer-Wilmes *Die Bedeutung der sogenannten Frauenfrage für die Kirchen und die Theologie. Eine (vor-) theologische Studie zur Erhellung des weiblichen Lebenszusammenhangs* (thesis: Münster 1979). I am indebted to this work as well as to C. J. M. Halkes.

15. Quoted by Meyer-Wilmes *Bedeutung, ibid.* p. 196; see *Declaration (Inter insignoires) on the Question of the Admission of Women to the Ministerial Priesthood* (C.T.S. 1976).

16. Hans Urs von Balthasar in the 'translator's foreword' to L. Boyer *Mystère et ministères de la femme* (Paris 1976), in the German version: *Frau und Kirche* (Einsiedeln 1977) p. 95.

17. See K. Völker (ed.) *Päpstin Johanna. Ein Lesebuch mit Texten vom Mittelalter bis heute* (Berlin 1977).

18. Foucault *Histoire*, cited in note 1.

19. As a theological-feminist joke has it: A particularly worthy man was allowed a preview of heavenly bliss. When he returned he was pale and upset. His friends anxiously inquired what God looked like. The virtuous man replied: 'She's black!'

20. I surely do not have to over-emphasise the fact that Marcuse refers to the opposite of that 'anthropological revolution' which Pier Paolo Pasolini describes as the mass impoverishment of institutionalised, uniform identities. See Pier Paolo Pasolini *Scritti Corsari* (Milan 1977).

21. See the conversation between S. Bovenschen and M. Schuller and Marcuse in *Gespräche mit Herbert Marcuse* (Frankfurt am Main 1978) pp. 65-87.

22. Marcuse *Gespräche ibid.* p. 83.

23. T. W. Adorno *Minima Moralia* (Frankfurt am Main 1969) p. 207.

c

Nadine Foley

Celibacy in the Men's Church

1. INTRODUCTION

TODAY THE ministerial priesthood of the Roman Catholic Church has been subjected to challenges on two of its traditional features, its maleness and its celibacy. The first is questioned by proponents of women's ordination to ministerial priesthood, the second primarily by priests themselves. The characteristics and dimensions of the women's ordination question today are a new phenomenon of Church history, and arise out of the contemporary movement for human liberation as it makes an impact upon the Church. The priestly celibacy issue, on the other hand, is not new, although the proportions of the current exodus of priests from their ministry is unprecedented. While celibacy is not the only factor accounting for this phenomenon, it is clearly one of them.[1] The two controverted areas have at least two things in common from the perspective of those who are asking the questions: (1) their starting point is experience; (2) *humanness* is the root issue. Despite the complexity of the two topics they come together on this basis and the commonality provides a reason for exploring the Church's views of women in relation to priestly celibacy.

The intent of this article is not to repeat what has already been thoroughly researched and published on the subject of priestly celibacy. In addition to the work of scholars,[2] there have been three authoritative Church statements on celibacy since 1967 beginning with the encyclical *Sacerdotalis Caelibatus*[3] of Pope Paul VI published in that year. The Synod of Bishops in their 1971 document on *The Ministerial Priesthood*[4] included a section on celibacy and on Holy Thursday 1979 Pope John

Paul II addressed the issue in his *Letter to Priests*.[5] The import of all three has been unequivocally to reaffirm the intent of the Roman Church to retain the requirement of celibacy for its priests.

What follows here pertains specifically to celibacy in relation to ministerial priesthood in so far as a juridical connection between the two has been maintained in the Western Church since the twelfth century. An ecclesial commitment to celibacy is not *per se* a commitment to ministerial priesthood as is evident in the tradition of non-clerical religious life. On the other hand ordination to priesthood canonically requires celibacy for the Roman Church. The association falls short of being intrinsic and necessary, since exceptions are granted in the case of ordained converts from various Christian communions and from the fact too that the Eastern Church, with certain limitations, has a married clergy. In the Western Church celibacy for ministerial priesthood is a matter of Church discipline and is imposed by law.

This fact does not imply that some in the ranks of ministerial priesthood do not choose celibacy as a preferred life option, as do those in religious life. Obviously, many do. They are the ones who value the celibate ideal and live it in open receptivity to all the facets of the human situation with an attitude of heart that does not admit of using and manipulating others, nor of imposing pre-determined restrictions upon personal relationships. But there is also evidence that for many priests, perhaps for the majority, celibacy is not a choice made but a condition accepted in the course of their preparation for priesthood. For some of these celibacy functions as a factor in personality maladjustment and spiritual disablement.[6] Their ministry is neither life-giving for them, nor for people around them. Accordingly, the real questions about celibacy arise in the existential arena of human inter-relationships as experienced by many priests and as perceived by those to whom they relate.

The contemporary exploration into the history, tradition, psychology, sociology, spirituality and juridical status of priestly celibacy has been occasioned by the ongoing debate about its relation to the priestly office. The official responses, of which Pope Paul VI's encyclical is the most comprehensive, set forth biblical and theological reasons for priestly celibacy, its ecclesial and eschatological significance, its relation to human values, as they offer principles for priestly formation, and admonitions against dangers to fidelity. One of the things that they do not address, something implicit in the rationale for priestly celibacy, is an ecclesial assessment of women which is institutionalised by the celibacy requirement for priests. This single facet of an admittedly intricate question, and one which may be apparent only to women, provides the vantage point for what follows. To pursue it will require a brief review of what the Church teaches about women.

2. THE CHURCH AND WOMEN

To the women who reads the various tracts on women in official Church publications critically, it soon becomes clear that the writers of these documents pursue their task in abstraction from the real world of women and in isolation from their contemporary experience. This is particularly regrettable since Pope John XXIII heralded the current age as one in which the aspirations of women, along with those of the economically and politically oppressed, point to the erosion of long sustained superiority-inferiority relations in which people have been held and to which the Church must be attentive.[7] Pope John rightly identified the new movements as arising out of the experience of people, a realisation which came to the surface dramatically in Vatican Council II when the conciliar fathers began to consider the situation of people in the Third World. Their bishops were men who shared their circumstances and participated in their misery. The bishops' eloquent testimony to the plight of their poor and destitute people, and to the Church's inadvertent complicity in the causes of the problems, made a major impact on the Council and radically changed its direction. The importance of experience as a *locus theologicus* was recognised then and it has been enunciated clearly in *The Evangelisation of the Modern World*.[8] The Church's emphases today on promoting the basic human rights of all people and on social justice as a constitutive element of the preaching of the Gospel grew out of attention to, and theological reflection upon, the experience of peoples who have been economically and politically oppressed.

The movement of women to achieve freedom in society and Church also has its basis in experience. But in this instance there is no channel of access through which their experience can reach the level at which Church doctrine and policy are formulated. Only women themselves are competent to speak to their own experience and they are systematically excluded from the exclusively male celibate hierarchical echelons. Yet there are those within these ranks who speak about them, to them, and for them. They are particularly persistent in repeating a kind of 'theology of women' which conceals within it an ancient *mythos* untouched by the findings of the contemporary sciences and completely disassociated from the experience of growing numbers of women.

In the various Church pronouncements women are consistently regarded as having a 'proper nature' and a 'specific role' to play in the human enterprise.[9] In his many affirmations of the need to promote the social, economic and political well-being of women in accord with developments taking place in the world today Pope Paul VI customarily added a qualification to the effect that women's 'proper role' must be safeguarded. In his allocution to the Italian Catholic Jurists in December

1972, Pope Paul indicated that which accounts for women's unique difference. 'Women's authentic liberation does not consist in a formalistic or materialistic equality with the other sex, but in recognising what the female personality has that is essentially specific to it: woman's vocation to be a mother.[10] Similarly, the conclusive argument of the *Declaration on the Question of the Admission of Women to the Ministerial Priesthood* centres around the notion of natures determining fixed roles. 'The whole sacramental economy is in fact based upon natural signs, on symbols printed on the human psychology. . . . The same natural resemblance is required for persons as for things: when Christ's role in the Eucharist is to be expressed sacramentally, there would not be this "natural resemblance" which must exist between Christ and his minister if the role of Christ were not taken by a man. In such a case it would be difficult to see in the minister the image of Christ. For Christ was and remains a man.'[11]

The language of *proper natures* and *specific roles* which pervades Church statements points to the scholastic categories which are employed. In that context the proper activity of anything is understood to be that differentiating activity which distinguishes the essence of something. Classically this was applied in fundamental Greek categories of being as in the Porphyrian tree. At the highest level of being in this schema the human individual was seen to be revealed through specific activities of rationality, functioning in the faculties of reason and will. These identified the human as distinct from the animal which at a lower level on the scale of being demonstrated the capabilities of sentiency and locomotion over what it held in common with lower organisms, i.e., plants.

While such principles are archaic in the light of more advanced biological science, they can be recalled here in an effort to understand exactly what is being said when such continued emphasis is placed upon motherhood as the proper role of women. There are a number of implications. When the elements of the Church discourse are considered in the scholastic context it seems to follow that the functions of rationality, i.e., reason and will, are the proper activity of males, while motherhood is the proper activity of females. What is proposed as the proper activity of women then is something which in the scale of being is shared with lower organisms. If this is a legitimate way of proceeding, one can conclude that there is not one human nature but two[12] and that of woman is obviously on a lower rung of the scale of being than that of men, even perhaps on a sub-human level. In effect then the official Church advances a two nature approach to human persons, with that of woman concentrated upon her biological role in procreation. If, as seemed to be the case in applying the scholastic categories, human nature is disclosed through the proper activities of reason and will, then by deduction, woman emerges as something less than fully human. To use the Freudian phrase, in her 'biology is destiny'. All of her potentialities as a human person, including reason and will if these are admitted, are conditioned by her child bearing function. This conclusion would appear to be inconsistent with the scholastic premises on which it is based since these did not distinguish males and females when speaking generically of human nature, although given the times in which scholasticism flourished the idea that women were fully human may never have been a consideration.

This brief effort to derive a conceptual framework in which to probe the meaning of what the Church is saying today about women may appear to be specious. Yet it seems to be legitimate, given the evidence. There is no claim here that philosophical analysis offers the *reason* for the position to which women are held in the Church and society. Rather the theoretical formulation is undoubtedly a rationalisation supporting ideas long held. It is not surprising in the light of the mediaeval theology which it reflects.[13] What is surprising is that it perpetuates for today suppositions unexamined in the light of an advanced biology, and the other human sciences. And it cloaks what are perhaps subconscious attitudes about women whose origins are even more ancient.

The source of ideas about women as inferior, defective, contaminated, seductive, and defiling human beings antedates Greek philosophy, of course. Primitive peoples the world over prohibited any kind of commerce with women before important male undertakings such as the hunt, negotiations of state, or warfare. Ancient cultures imposed blood tabus and segregated women from cultic celebrations because of their presumed capacity for violating the sacred. Contact with women, particularly sexual intercourse, was generally held to be a source of pollution and debilitation for the male. In the conscious and unconscious levels of cultural conditioning these attitudes and the practices which flowed from them attest to the long persistence of an underlying fear of woman, associated with her biological processes, especially her motherhood, her perceived relation to the earth and its fertility, and her occult power over males.[14]

The question for many Catholic women today is whether or not their Church perceives that the incarnation of Jesus Christ has in fact radically changed their status. In the many tracts on the complementarity of women's roles with those of men, on the indispensable, even exclusive, role of motherhood which women are called upon to exercise in the family, society and culture, and on the inestimable qualities of the female personality, they detect, not a doctrine of women which frees and promotes their individual personhood, but rather a subtle 'theological' reinforcement of unexamined premises about women that are not compatible with their emergent self concepts.

In an age when women are rightfully claiming their full human personhood with all its attendant implications for participation in social, economic and political life, they come up against an ecclesial doctrine which is not consonant with their developing self identity. To women it appears that the long maintained insistence upon their *roles*, and that word is significant, ignores the more important question of who women *are*, i.e., human persons with unique complements of characteristics and gifts. Even before women are mothers, they are persons with their own identities. Motherhood, however noble, does not supersede personhood, but both in theory and in effect, the notion that women find all their identity and fulfilment in motherhood, either natural or spiritual, has been operative. It has been internalised by women and men and both have been diminished in the process. Today many women and men are acknowledging that fact and turning to the process of self-discovery unencumbered by the stereotyped patterns of gender expectations. They are mining a rich store of data for examination in the light of the gospel with which their experience resonates in its message of freedom. And they offer to the Church an immense new potential for probing the meaning of the gospel centred in the person of Jesus Christ.

On the other hand what the Church offers women and declares to the world at large is a veiled rationale for a secondary status wherein they are controlled, protected and prevented from sharing fully in the effects of the incarnation. In so doing the Church substantiates the premises of patriarchy and the superiority-inferiority relationships it perpetuates in all forms of society. The contradiction to the gospel message of redemption is experienced by increasing numbers of women as frustration and embarrassment. They find themselves victims of an ideology embodied in the ecclesiastical structure which provides them no recourse. Priestly celibacy is both a symbolic expression of the predicament and a real barrier to its resolution.

3. PRIESTLY CELIBACY AND WOMEN, SYMBOL AND BARRIER

Priestly celibacy is a unique symbol of women's relation to the patriarchal Church. Patriarchal societies generally institutionalise their concepts of women. The Church, which declares itself to be a unique society, one 'original in her nature and structures',[15] does so singularly when it associates celibacy with priesthood and thus with authority and the exercise of power in the Church. The Church, the body of Christ, is *holy*. Its rites are *sacred*. It is in the nature of *sacrament*. It is *the house of God* and *the dwelling place of God among men, filled with heavenly gifts for all* eternity. These phrases are among those used in *Lumen Gentium* to describe the supernatural character and mission of the Church.[16]

Similar allusions occur when priesthood is described. Ordination to priesthood is *sacred*. While all the faithful are made a 'holy and kingly priesthood' in Christ, some men among them 'hold in the community of the faithful the sacred power of order, that of offering sacrifice and forgiving sin'. Clearly ministerial priesthood adds to the holiness of the people of God, the capacity for the exercise of sacred power 'joined with the episcopal order the office of priest shares in the authority by which Christ builds up and sanctifies and rules his Body'. By the special character conferred in the sacrament of orders priests by the anointing of the Holy Spirit 'are configured to Christ the priest in such a way that they are able to act in the person of the head'.[17]

In his encyclical *Sacerdotalis Caelibatus* Pope Paul VI speaks of the sacred celibacy of the clergy, the golden law of sacred celibacy, the perfect chastity of the Church's ministers which is 'particularly suited' to God's ministers. In contrast to marriage which has been elevated and sacramentalised by Jesus, he also 'opened a new way, in which the human creature adheres wholly and directly to the Lord, and is concerned only with him, and with his affairs'.[18] 'The consecrated celibacy of the sacred ministers actually manifests the virginal love of Christ for the Church, and the virginal and supernatural fecundity of this marriage, by which the children of God are born 'not of blood, nor of the will of the flesh'.[19] Pope John Paul II carries this idea even further when he states that the priest by renouncing the fatherhood proper to married men 'seeks another fatherhood, even another motherhood, recalling the words of the apostle about the children he begets in suffering'.[20]

When a woman reads sequentially in this way descriptions of the holiness of the Church, the sacral character of the ministerial priesthood and the sacredness of celibacy she is keenly aware that she has little or no place in the discourse, and she cannot help but infer that her exclusion relates to prescriptions about the realm of the sacred. While she can assume that she belongs to the people of God who are called holy, perusal of other Church statements, written and translated in a repetitive masculine idiom,[21] may cause her to doubt even this concession. In tracts on priesthood she has no place and when celibacy is the issue she is aware that she inhabits the shadowy periphery of the discussion especially when the priest is admonished about the temptations to infidelity against which he must take precaution.

One obvious meaning of celibacy in ecclesial discourse is 'unmarried to a woman'. Although negative in form, as opposed to the considerable material that is proposed as the positive content and value of celibacy, this connotation is critical for women. If the special character of the Church, its priests, and their celibacy is sacredness, and if a non-celibate state is inappropriate to sacred priesthood, despite the tradition of the eastern Church, then something definitive is being said about women and about marital relations with women. *Women are unfit to approach the realm of the sacred or the person of the sacred minister*. Furthermore, sexual intercourse defiles the sacred minister and renders him inapt for his priestly function.[22] Church documents do not state these things in so many words but they are inescapable conclusions from what is concealed behind the rationale for priestly celibacy and the rhetoric of proper natures, specific roles, and women's complementary relation to man.[23] They suggest that the Church has not really accepted the meaning of what happened when Jesus became one like us, women and men, in everything except sin.

Institutionalised celibacy effectively distances women from the priestly caste and stands as an implicit statement that the Church in its hier-archical expression has no need of women. Inadvertently no doubt, Pope John Paul II reinforces this conclusion when he suggests that through renouncing fatherhood the priest seeks 'another fatherhood and even another motherhood', which latter activity elsewhere he calls 'the eternal vocation of women'.[24] How does such a strange statement of androgyny account for 'symbols imprinted on the human psychology?' If priesthood should in some way incorporate, symbolise and function as motherhood, how much more appropriate might it be to ordain women.

The fact that sacred celibacy is wedded to Church authority creates an impenetrable barrier to open dialogue on the many issues related to women and their full membership and participation in the Church. Women's own experience of themselves as individual human persons with unique gifts and capabilities is the conclusive evidence refuting the long prevailing ecclesial attitudes. While slow and painstaking inroads are being made by women in the secular social, economic and political spheres, comparable possibilities simply do not exist in the Church. There is no forum within the official Church for theological reflection based upon the experience of women. The structures of ecclesial patriarchy are insulated against such an endeavour and many women are frustrated by the continued affront to their personhood which they experience in trying to address the inequities which persist within the Church.

The issue is clearly one of power and the consequences of the exercise of power. The word *power* used in reference to women's motivation in seeking their full equality is universally disturbing to men. The classic denigration of the women's liberation movement is the disdainful accusa-tion by men that women are only trying to gain power. While the word has sinister overtones in a feminine context, it should be appreciated for the reality that it is. Fundamental power is that which is exercised in control of one's own life, whether exercised personally or in concert with others. It is bound up with recognition that one is fully a person. This is the power that women seek in the wider women's movement and in that aspect of it which addresses their position in the Church. In one respect the problem touches all lay persons, but it affects women in a singular manner.

While the laity generally are unenfranchised in the Church, women, as an undifferentiated class, are doubly excluded. No woman can pass over the line of demarcation between clergy and laity. It is curious then that in the aftermath of official pronouncements on women in ministerial priest-hood, there should be protestations of the need to involve women in decision-making.[25] All significant Church decision-making is carried out at the upper echelons of celibate Church hierarchy in which even the lower clergy has little influence and from which women are categorically barred.

The current experience of women continues to bear out that reality. Women may not bring their concerns directly to national conferences of bishops. Leaders of religious congregations of women find avenues for discussion of mutual concerns with bishops blocked while unilateral episcopal decisions are made affecting their well-being. Women of superior professional preparation and experience continue to serve in positions subordinate to those of less qualified priests in diocesan offices. Women are told by high ranking Church officials that they do not have the competence to participate in projects such as the revision of canon law for religious institutes, and that they have not the kind of judgment required for an adjudicatory role on a marriage tribunal.

When new liturgical roles are opened for the laity, the intent is to make them available to lay *men*. The decree, *Ministeria Quaedam*,[26] is a case in point. Women are prohibited from joining the ranks of acolytes, lectors, extraordinary ministers, permanent deacons and preachers. In a pat-ronising vein they are told that 'the Church owes both lay and religious women its own great debt of gratitude for their commitment and loving service'[27] a particularly telling kind of assertion in so far as it sets women outside 'the Church'. In that sense it is an honest statement of the *status quo* as women experience it. The litany of repressive experiences could continue.

Certainly there are breakthroughs in many of the specific areas es-pecially in local situations and among persons, men and women, priests, religious and laity, who are growing in sensitivity to the fundamental injustice. Extraordinary precedents are set in some instances where pas-toral needs are critical. The document, *The Role of Women in Evangel-isation*, records that in mission fields women administer parishes, preach, baptise, and witness marriages.[28] In these cases, under the pressure of priest shortages, the advance of women parallels what is slowly taking place in society at large. But in the Church this development can proceed only so far. A line is drawn beyond which there is no trespass and it is epitomised by the male celibate priesthood.

The concessions that are granted to women are exceptional and condescending. They do nothing to alleviate the radical disparity of which women are acutely aware when they encounter it internalised by the members of the élite sacerdotal corps. Everything in the training of priests has supported them in what is perhaps an unconscious realisation, i.e., that they never have to relate to a woman as a peer. From this fact flows an ingrained attitude towards women as inferiors which customarily expresses itself in clerical domination and patronage on the one hand and in reassuring praise for the feminine estate on the other. In this antifeminist mentality of priests the formal Church teaching about women reaches into the ordinary circumstances where women interact with members of the clergy. More and more frequently these situations are the ones in which priests and women, lay and religious, are engaging in ministry. The results are often painful for the persons involved and irreparably damaging to the ministry.

This area can only be addressed adequately by priests themselves, but there is evidence that the so-called 'crisis of priesthood' is at its roots a crisis of human identity, the consequence of the inflexible tie between authority and celibacy as it functions in their lives. On the experimental level many priests realise in effect the import of what Schillebeeckx maintains when he says, 'Celibacy is not the sort of thing that one can take on because one has to go along with something else'.[29]

In a perceptive article on celibacy Rodger Balducelli traces its biblical foundation in the teaching of Jesus and the genesis of the decision for celibacy in those who make it. He describes how the reality of the kingdom of God so possesses a person that the decision for celibacy flows from an existential inability to choose otherwise. The choice 'because of the kingdom of God' (Matt. 19:21) is interpreted by Balducelli as a case of celibacy capturing the individual rather than of a person's making a deliberated option for celibacy so as to dedicate themselves to the kingdom to come. 'The event of celibacy is intelligible as one that comes about within a major religious experience and as an existential repercussion of it.'[30] If then a choice of celibacy occurs within the preferential realm of a person's relationship with God, it cannot be commandeered, either by the individual or by anyone else. It certainly cannot be legislated. It is, of course, possible that persons who aspire to priesthood are also impelled to the choice of celibacy by the intervention of God in their lives. But should that not be the case, celibacy is for them a legality, carrying with it the prohibition of marriage, and the necessity of shoring up their defences against the presumed dangers that women represent. A ready consequence for the priest which has sometimes been published under the guise of 'pastoral psychology'[31] is a tendency to disparage sex and women. The extent to which covertly and even overtly they speak and act out of such a set mind is known only to priests but it can be intuited by women.

The consequences of celibate patriarchy are uniquely experienced by priests and they are a source of anguished personal stress to many. Psychological and sociological studies have been done which indicate the damage done to the personality of many priests whose commitment to celibacy closes off the experience of human intimacy. But the priest is also locked into a system of control which effectively contains him and at the same time requires him to be an unparticipative spokesperson for an authoritarian Church policy legislated from above. In close contact with the pastoral needs of people he often finds himself in conflictive situations with no authority to deal sensitively with destructive human problems of people.[32] When this happens the priest himself experiences depersonalisation in his own way and comes to know the effects of patriarchy on those who function in the lowest strata.

Insights into this phenomenon come from men who, as a consequence of the women's movement, have begun to explore the sources of their own oppression.[33] Joseph H. Pleck has written on the ways in which power in patriarchy affects women, men, and society. He notes that under patriarchy 'men's relationships with other men cannot help but be shaped and patterned by patriarchal norms, though they are less obvious than the norms governing male-female relationships'.[34] What these norms are in the celibate patriarchal Church priests can discover through consciousness-raising efforts. But it is obvious that advancement comes to those who internalise the values of the institution in the most exemplary manner and accordingly are called to higher office. In secular patriarchies the rankings correspond to criteria for masculinity as the society identifies them. In the Church, where celibacy diminishes the potential for 'masculinity' in the secular male-prescribed senses, levels of authority are still indicative of degrees of power. Those on the lowest rungs of the hierarchical ladder are the least empowered and in fact are closest to the female status of 'underclass' which every patriarchy requires. Given the standards by which any patriarchy functions this is an uncomfortable position for men to be in, and priests are no exception. It should be no surprise then that when priests want to open up a dialogue on celibacy in the Church they are caught in the strange web that is woven from the strands of celibacy and authority. And in this instance they share with women the experience of having no recourse. They are denied by higher authority the possibility of participating in a decision on celibacy. Consequently, there is no way that their experience can become a *locus theologicus* which as a basis for reflection might open the Church to new levels of ecclesial understanding and new expressions of the manner in which Jesus Christ has effected the freedom of his disciples.

In the final analysis the real issue which underlies the problems about women and priestly celibacy for the Church is its witness to the incarnation in its members and in its ecclesial organisation for ministry. And obviously the core of the matter is human sexuality, an area which still stands in need of a solid theological foundation benefiting from the insights developed in over a century of study by the human sciences, and offering a new ethical orientation for the vexing problems people face in the confused moral climate of this era. Unfortunately, until that work is done and implemented in the Church, a project in which women must be directly involved, difficulties about women and about priestly celibacy in relation to ministry will persist, and unnecessary restrictions will continue to limit the potential of the Church to bear witness to Christ in the world.

In their document, *The Role of Women in Evangelisation*, the Vatican Congregation for the Evangelisation of Peoples wrote: 'It is certain that sisters often suffer deeply at the sight of the neglected state of Christian communities, threatened by loss of vitality and death. Their requests to be entrusted with greater pastoral responsibilities spring from this anguish and not from a spirit of pretension, and should be examined with sympathy and with the urgency required by the circumstances.'[35] Despite their reference to 'sisters' what these words describe is shared by many women and men who look for ways in which to be more fully involved in the Church's ministry. But sexual and celibate barriers impede them from becoming communicators of the healing, reconciling, and celebrating love of Jesus Christ in the world. And the potential of the Church to carry out its mission is thereby limited. The 'urgency required by the circumstances' is great, but for the Church's leaders it is not great enough yet to open up the dialogue, to listen to their own members and discover what great reserves of ministry are ready and available for the work of evangelisation.

As numbers of those in the priestly ranks dwindle, and as more and more highly motivated women become disenchanted with a Church which segregates them and keeps them at a distance, the Church loses valuable personnel to be sure. But it loses something even greater and that is its credibility as a witness to one who came that 'all might have life and have it more abundantly' (John 10:10). What remains is the highly visible celibate patriarchal Church embodying its own message of intransigence before the spirit-endowed gifts of its own members and before the world of real women and men for whom even today the Word became flesh.

Notes

1. See 'The Discussion on Celibacy' *The Identity of the Priest, Concilium* 43 ed. Karl Rahner (1969) 136-174; and *Celibacy in the Church, Concilium* 78, ed. William Bassett and Peter Huizing (1972).

2. See, for example, the documentation in the two aforementioned volumes of *Concilium* and in works such as Edward Schillebeeckx, *Celibacy* trans. C. A. L. Jarrott (1968).

3. *The Pope Speaks* (Autumn 1967) 291-319; *A.A.S.* 59 (1967) 657-697.

4. (Washington, D.C: United States Catholic Conference 1972) 4 pp. 22-25; *A.A.S.* 63 (1972) 897 ff.

5. *Origins* 8 (19 April 1979) 696-704.

6. See Eugene Kennedy 'Stress in Ministry—an Overview' *Chicago Studies* 18 (Spring 1979) 10-11.

7. *Pacem in Terris* (Washington, D.C.: United States Catholic Conference 1963) p. 11; *A.A.S.* 55 (1963) 267-268.

8. (Washington, D.C.: United States Catholic Conference 1973) p. 10; A.A.S. 68 (1976) 5-76.

9. See my article 'Woman in Vatican Documents 1960 to the Present' *Sexism and Church Law* ed. James Coriden (New York 1977) pp. 82-108.

10. 'The Right to Be Born' *The Pope Speaks* 17 (Winter 1973) 335.

11. *Origins* 6 (3 February 1977) 522; *A.A.S.* 69 (1977) 98-116.

12. See also André Guindon 'L'Être femme: deux lectures': *Église and Théologie* (January 1978) 111-121.

13. See Eleanor Como McLaughlin 'Equality of Souls, Inequality of Sexes: Woman in Medieval Theology' *Religion and Sexism* ed. Rosemary Radford Reuther (New York) pp. 213-266.

14. See Wolfgang Lederer *The Fear of Women* (New York 1968).

15. *Declaration on the Question of the Admission of Women to the Ministerial Priesthood* cited in note 11 at p. 513.

16. *Dogmatic Constitution on the Church, Vatican II. The Conciliar and Post Conciliar Documents*, ed. Austin Flannery (Newport 1975) pp. 350-358 *et passim.*

17. *Decree on the Ministry and Life of Priests, op. cit.* pp. 865-868 *et passim.*

18. *op. cit.* 20, p. 297.

19. *op. cit.* 26, p. 299.

20. 'Letter to Priests' cited in note 5.

21. The English translation of Pope John Paul II's encyclical, *Redemptor Hominis*, is a case in point. See *Origins* 8 (22 March 1979) 625-643.

22. See 'Celibacy, Canon Law and Synod 1971' *Celibacy in the Church* p. 114, where James Coriden has summarised the remarks of Cardinal Enrique y Tarancon to the 1971 Synod of Bishops. The cardinal explicitly stated that the Church does not demand the charism of celibacy for reasons of 'ritualistic purity'. Yet in the past this was definitely the case and from a woman's perspective appears still to be operative. On the background of 'cultic purity', see E. Schillebeeckx, *Celibacy* 57-58.

23. Demetrios Constantelos states '. . . emphasis on celibacy hides inherently

and subconsciously the patriarchal concept which degrades women into a secondary position or sees her as the means through which sin was introduced into the world'. 'Marriage and Celibacy of the Clergy in the Orthodox Church' *Celibacy in the Church* p. 36.

24. See 'Allocution to a General Audience' *L'Osservatore Romano* (English edition) N. 3 (564) 15 January 1979 p. 9.

25. Archbishop Joseph Bernardin 'Statement' *Women in Catholic Priesthood: an Expanded Vision* ed. Anne Marie Gardiner (New York 1976) p. 195.

26. 'The Ministries of Lector and Acolyte' *The Pope Speaks* 17 (Autumn 1972) pp. 257-261. After citing the desire of Mother Church to lead 'all the faithful' into full, conscious and active participation in liturgical celebrations, norm 7 reads: 'In accordance with the venerable tradition of the Church, installation in the ministries of acolyte and lector is reserved to men' *op. cit.* p. 261.

27. Archbishop Joseph Bernardin in the Statement cited in note 25 at p. 197.

28. Issued by the Pastoral Commission of the Vatican Congregation for the Evangelisation of Peoples, *Origins* 5 (22 April 1976) pp. 702-707. See also Katherine Gilfeather 'The Changing Role of Women in the Catholic Church in Chile' *Journal for the Scientific Study of Religion* 16 (March 1977) 39-54.

29. *Celibacy* p. 120.

30. 'Decision for Celibacy' *Theological Studies* 36 (June 1975) 227-228.

31. A particularly distressing instance is Willibald Demal *Pastoral Psychology in Practice* trans. Joachim Werner Conway (New York 1955) pp. 54-65.

32. See Richard A. Schoenherr 'Holy Power? Holy Authority? and Holy Celibacy?' *Celibacy in the Church* pp. 234-235; and Cletus Wessels 'Priests' Liberation' *Priests for Equality* July 1979 pp. 1-4.

33. For a review of the literature of this movement see James B. Harrison 'Men's Roles and Men's Lives' *Signs: Journal of Women in Culture and Society* 4 (No. 2 1978) 324-336.

34. 'Men's Power with Women, Other Men and Society: a Men's Movement Analysis' *Women and Men: the Consequences of Power* (Cincinnati, Ohio: Office of Women's Studies, University of Cincinnati 1976) p. 16.

35. Cited in note 28, at p. 705.

PART II

The Situation Today

Elizabeth Carroll

Can Male Domination be Overcome?

T. S. ELIOT has written, 'Every moment is a new and shocking valuation of all we have been'.[1] The title of this article presents a particularly shocking moment of valuation. The question, 'Can male domination be overcome?' assumes male domination as a fact, assumes that it is an evil, and assumes that it may be inevitable. This paper will attempt to nuance the first assumption, demonstrate the second, present reasons for discounting the third, and give a positive response to the central question. These questions will be addressed by surveying contemporary data of the social and behavioural sciences, reflecting upon the data in the light of Christian anthropology, and outlining possible action orientations towards a social body more capable of mutuality and love.

1. THE FACT

Domination designates that basic principle of society and of individual behaviour which assumes that the fundamental glue of human relationships is the right of some groups to control other groups, or some individuals to control others because they are members of those groups. These groups usually differ from the dominant in race, national origin, class, religion or sex. All domination results from human inability to deal with differences in any way except through the imposition of power. The 'different' is categorised as the inferior, and some form of dependency relationship imposed. Structures of dominance are ordinarily hierarchical.[2]

Behaviours associated with domination can range from violence or the threat of violence to the put-down or debilitating stare. But the most insidious and harmful is the structural form of domination which organises society, the economy, political life, and religion in ways which exclude the subordinated group from participation in the fruits of the enterprise and/or its decision-making. To support this form of domination, an ideology is constructed to rationalise the way things are. With time, the system and its ideology, prejudiced though they may be in promoting the interests of the dominant and dehumanising the subordinate, become accepted as 'the way things are' or even 'the way things are meant to be'.

Male domination applies the basic principle of domination in terms of sex. Its origins have been sought in varieties of physiological, psychological and social data, including differences in physical strength, incomplete knowledge of human procreative processes, primitive fears and sexual fantasies of men, and the excessive busyness of women in combining domestic and productive roles.

Some socio-biologists trace male domination to the most primitive stage of human history and even to the behaviour of primates. Differences of physical strength are perceived as basic.[3] Many conscientious researchers today conclude on the other hand, that in the gatherer/hunter era of human history, egalitarian patterns may have prevailed, in which the physical strength of men was not the sole determinant of worth, but where 'the cognitive-analytic, the symbolic-aesthetic, and the social-bonding talents of both women and men are fully developed and fully exercised'.[4]

During the neolithic period the awesome role of woman in human fertility and in the discovery of agriculture seems to have dominated social thought, so that the worship of the Mother Goddess became a major cultural force, and women had 'their moment in history'.[5] With the age of metals, iron ploughs and iron weapons emphasised the difference in physical strength of men and women. Wars of conquest for 'seizing wealth rather than creating it' were accompanied by the introduction of myths of the Warrior Gods who displaced, transformed or obliterated the Mother Goddesses.[6] Men had become cognisant of the male role in human conception, and tended to see the woman as merely the depository and nurturer of the all powerful male seed.[7]

Urbanisation in particular, with its stratified social roles, brought reductions of woman's status. As Elise Boulding puts it: the city 'contains all kinds of material possessions, and it *contains* women—but it seems to *launch* men'.[8] Woman space became constricted, especially for that urban creation, women of the middle classes. The constriction of woman space to the domestic did not keep poor women out of the mills and mines and factories, but it did continue their special treatment in terms of poor conditions and low pay. When women work outside the home, they also have the burdens, psychological and laborious, of household and family. So important is the double work load that Boulding feels it may have been a central reason why women were able to be excluded from the sphere of public policy.[9] Even today, throughout the world, in socialist and capitalist, 'developing' and industrial countries, the average salary for working women is less than two thirds that of men. The number of women who neither read nor write far exceeds the number of men so limited.[10] Without literacy women lack that ability to criticise in ways that may transform their societies. On the other hand public role and positions of public responsibility in political, economic and religious spheres only very slowly are opening to women even after they have broken through the educational barriers. The segregation of female roles from public life which became established in early historical times of city and empire, has continued, with exceptions and in varying degrees, till the present. Patriarchy brought the blessing of religious authority to this structure.

The Church coming out of a tradition of patriarchy, Jewish law, particularly in the period of Jesus' earthly mission, saw no place for women except in domestic roles. Woman achieved status not in her own personhood, but through marriage and childbearing.[10] God's covenant with the Hebrew people was symbolised in the circumcision of males, but not at all in women. Women had no responsibility to the daily or temple prayers, were excluded from study, including the Torah. Women could not bear witness, and were expected not to speak in public even to their husbands and certainly not to a rabbi. It was in this environment in which the Jewish man formally thanked God each day for not having been born a woman that Jesus ministered. Jesus provided the redemptive grace to 'make all things new'[11] for woman as for man. Yet through a few rabbinically influenced passages of St Paul and patristic commentary the established cultural stereotypes prevailed. Christians, despite the example of Jesus' treatment of women, became embroiled in the dichotomous stereotypes of woman as the temptress and woman as the paragon of virtue.

2. THE EVIL

Although even the gross injustice of slavery went unquestioned by Church and synagogue at one time, it would be difficult for a committed believer today to deny that slavery, oppression and alienation are evil. Recent theological trends as divergent as personalism, liberation theology, biography as theology and human experience as bespeaking the movement of the Holy Spirit reinforce the conviction that refusal to discover, affirm and promote the gifts of all is sinful.[12]

Power applied as domination is evil since it loses its potential as a tool for freeing others and organising their creative capacities and contributions for their own and for the common good. Power becomes the enforcement of the will of the dominant person or group upon the subordinate. Role, character, and virtue of the subordinate are defined by the dominant in order that the subordinate may serve the ends of the dominant. Domination, in other words, prevents self-definition. It imposes an ideology which divides people and their activities into the important and the negligible, the recorded and the absentees of history. It judges persons not in terms of their contributions to the well-being of society but in terms of that set mind which has already categorised them as 'in' or 'outside of' the pale of the dominant. In these ways domination distorts truth.

In the case of male domination, traditions have developed which have not only excluded women from public and sacred space and from the cultivation of skills and intellect associated with leadership roles, but have subordinated them even in domestic régimes. To justify these structures of dominance, an ideology of male supremacy has firmly established the secret pervasive 'assumption that men are the ones who matter and that women exist only in relation to them'.[13] 'Men are seen as powerful, active, self-sufficient and fully human; women as weak, passive and dependent support players in the essentially male drama. Male nature is human nature, female nature is to be helpmeet to man.'[14] 'Feminine' qualities are conceived as not merely different from masculine, but are defined relative to the male's, as their opposite or negative. Rationality is assigned to men: intuition, nurturing, sensitivity to women. Because these traits are thus assigned, sexual domination dictates that rationality is considered essential, and that traits described as feminine are secondary.[15]

Chauvinism has through the ages created a morass of contradictory generalisations about women. In philosophy, law and theology, 'the examined life' is the male life. Woman may thus be defined by St Thomas Aquinas as 'defective and misbegotten' and described as lacking 'eminence'.[16] Because a male/female, superior/inferior approach (expanded by Greek dualism into spirit/flesh) enters into the most intimate sphere of human relations, it poisons at the source, in both the male and the female, the human potential for mutuality. It imposes upon most women a sense of inferiority which, over centuries, has been deeply interiorised.[17] The false superiority and psychological demand to be always in control meanwhile weigh upon men even in a physically destructive way. To the extent that the Church loses sight of the truth that both men and women have one main role, that of being human, and looks at women only through 'their full proper *role* in accordance with *their own nature*'[18] the Church is inviting women to a false self image; a distortion of God's creation. On one hand such phrases remind one of St Thomas Aquinas'

'Woman is defective' definition. On the other hand they tend to extol in women qualities which should be characteristic of *all* sensitive Christians, e.g., intuition, creativity, sensibility, a sense of piety and compassion, a profound capacity for understanding and love.[19]

Moreover the fullness of this human role is denied by such anomalies as refusing to them installation into the *lay* ministries of acolyte and lector or admission to the testing of their call to ordained ministry, in the name of a much flawed 'tradition'.[20] Far from helping women to throw off their inferiority complex, the Church deepens it also by the use of exclusive language in its liturgy (seeming to ignore the presence of women).

Sexual domination, moreover, provides a paradigm for other forms of domination. The patterns built into the human psyche through male domination promote and legitimise racism, classism, religious hostility, aggressive nationalism and imperialism, as well as individual mani-festations of prejudice. Domination breeds dehumanisation for the dominant as for the subjugated. Consciousness of this evil has been raised. Its continuance, in Judaeo-Christian terminology, is sin.

3. INEVITABILITY

Since the examples of male domination are so continuous in the experi-ence of both society and religions, the conclusion seems inevitable that nothing can be done to change matters. Some contemporary claims are made that sex differences necessarily resulting in dominance-dependency relations are innate, built into the human genes, and hence irreversible. Some sociobiologists contend, largely through the study of primates (ethology) extrapolated to the human, that males are born aggressive, females nurturant and dependent, as a result of instincts inherited from remote prehuman creatures.[21] It is argued that the genetic code (of XX chromosomes for women, and XY chromosomes for men) and the result-ing hormonal secretions make every cell of a man's body different from every cell of a woman's body. Best-sellers popularise the idea that men possess genetic imprints which drive them to be aggressive, to bond with one another, and to dominate. Work differences are ascribed to biologi-cal differences.[22]

This conclusion is rejected by most scientific workers today who limit biological imperatives to those sex differences related immediately to the production of new human life. Other sex differences promote the co-operation necessary. It is the *patterns* of co-operation which give rise to gender stereotypes, and no particular gender stereotype is unalterable.[23]

While it is true that both genetic endowment and prenatal influences offset every person's physical health and mental capacity, only two sex-differentiated psychological traits seem to be strongly genetically determined: greater aggressiveness and better visual-spatial ability in males.[24] And cross-cultural studies indicate that even the latter trait is more apparent in strongly dominant-dependent relations than where both sexes are allowed independence in early life.[25] Field studies by careful anthropologists have called attention, to significant differences between men's and women's roles in many societies. They indicate that patterns result 'from features of the social structure which have been elicited by a particular culture'.[26]

Some religious determinists ignore the sociobiologists' evolutionary theses, but do rely heavily on gender stereotypes and fundamentalist interpretations of the Scriptural texts, especially of St Paul, to impose the domination of men over women as part of the natural order of creation and of divine law. If the isolated texts supporting this vein are placed in context of other texts and of the gospel message, however, they lose their impact.[27] If any attitude of Jesus is clear from his almost defiant use of the Sabbath for working miracles, it is that human beings were not made for the Sabbath, but the Sabbath for them.[28] In instance after instance Jesus is shown dialoguing freely with,[29] blessing the initiative and work of women,[30] praising deviation from their set roles.[31] So changed was Jesus' attitude towards women from what was approved for Jews, that Christian practice, unlike the Jewish law which allowed God's Covenant to be represented only in the male through circumcision, admitted woman as her own person to baptism. Baptism is the seal of the Holy Spirit on personhood, and should carry with it the acknowledgment of full human autonomy, those qualities of intellect, freedom, creativity, and power of love which mark male and female as image of God. Catholic tradition has strongly rejected the doctrine of predestination that human nature is radically perverted by the results of original sin, and has emphasised free will.[32] Vatican Council II extolled freedom, for 'the Lord himself came to free and strengthen man, renewing him inwardly and casting out the prince of this world'.[33] Not even the long-continued tradition of male domination is inevitable if men and women accept the redemptive power of Jesus to effect change.

4. POSITIVE IMPULSES

Male domination can be overcome. There are in motion already formative influences which will alter society and Church. The first is the consciousness of male domination as a sinful human structure, which can be abolished; the second is the growing success of women and men in altering personal and social relationships. Renewal will not be deep and thorough unless it is based upon a revolution of consciousness, that 'gestalt shift in the whole way of seeing our relations to one another, so that our behaviour patterns are re-formed from inside out'.[34] Consciousness is a grace. Every advance in consciousness means a growing attention to the presence of the Spirit of God working in people and events, to reveal a reality which, through familiarity, has gone unnoticed. It is the change of behaviour patterns that Jesus' life was about. From the first word of public preaching, as Mark portrays it, Jesus calls for conversion, repentance.[35] He displaces biological ties to lay bare the fundamental capacity of human beings—women and men alike—to do the will of God, and thus become his 'brother and sister and mother'.[36] Continually he rejects domination as the pattern for his disciples: 'Whoever wants to be great among you will be your servant.'[37] Through such teachings Jesus laid the basis for a Christian doctrine of personhood, a concept that could not penetrate the established customs of male domination wrought by patriarchy and the dualistic system of thought, but which remained as the ideal to be reinstated through an expansion of human consciousness.[38] The thinking that guided Vatican Council II stressed the concepts that 'we are all members of one people, without distinctions based on sex or race, the dignity of each person is to be fostered in terms of unity and liberty, in the perspective of a new creation to be brought to fulfilment in Christ'.[39] The Church thus has within its doctrinal armoury the universal moral principles needed to conquer male domination. The essential step is to bring these principles into concrete application through consciousness, conviction and conversion.

The promotion of consciousness to male domination is looked upon by many, however, as a divisive activity, as a destroyer of innocence, an awakening in women of hurts and angers, of rage at the justification and continuation of unjust situations and structures. For the anger to be redemptive it must be recognised, struggled with in terms of the over-arching command and power, generated by Christ's sacrifice, to love. The result will be a love which is based on reality, not sentimentality, a love out of which real co-operativeness and mutuality can develop because they are based on honesty. Changes incorporating these values already characterise the lives of many young men and women, who establish mutuality in their life plans. They draw up pre-marital contracts which stress equality in resources and in decision-making, mutual consultation before making changes which will affect the other; retention of her maiden name by the woman to enhance her sense of self; and men's assumption of nurturing roles with children. 'Flexi-time' working hours to free both men and women for child care are becoming available. The prevalence of co-education, the legal requirements for 'Affirmative Action' in education, sports, hiring, promotion, and salary are gradually altering society and business.

Congregations of religious women have for the last decade been experimenting with non-hierarchic international government structures. Collegiality and subsidiarity broaden the base of decision-making to affect every member, calling forth their initiative, faith and generosity in ways that contribute to their growth in human qualities of freedom and responsibility. In the same way women need to be encouraged to bring the long-neglected riches of their personalities and their long-hidden corporate cultural potential to bear upon their national political units and their Church. As women bearing gifts gain welcome in the secular society,[40] they will reject any artificial subordination imposed by the Church.

As Boulding maintains, redirection of human persons is far from hopeless. She finds a chief reason for optimism in the fact that the old structures are not working any more. The immense changes wrought in our world by science, cybernetics, communication, transportation were wrought by human beings conscious of their power. United Nations Conferences stress that it is only lack of *will* that prevents a better world from being realised. Women and men are today newly conscious of the immense dangers to human survival inherent in their aggressive attitudes towards one another, especially as these attitudes are empowered by nuclear weapons, by economic exploitation, and by terrorism. Because most decisions leading to this state of affairs have been male decisions, women constitute the great untapped potential for society and Church. If women have even a small share of the virtues that have been attributed to their 'feminine nature', it is time that these be freed from protective chains and made available to our world. The Church can aid this process immensely by bringing to bear the full riches of its teaching, its authoritative resources and its structural reform in support of women's efforts 'to claim [their] rights as marks of [their] dignity'.[41]

If Genesis 1:27 is to be taken seriously, the image of God and the responsibility to image God are entrusted to both male and female. If the gospel of Jesus is to be taken seriously, the liberation of women counts among the most basic mandates of the messianic mission. Wary though the disciples may be of their ability to be faithful in extending this mission to all the as yet disenfranchised, their hope is that the gospel is empowerment and that the truth will set all free. Immense are the implications of *Populorum Progressio*, in saying that persons are as responsible for their development as they are for salvation.[42] Having begun to unleash the human potential that is denied expression wherever domination exists, men and women are realising that this is a godly beginning, bringing near the reign of God.

Notes

1. T. S. Eliot *Four Quartets* (New York 1943) p. 26.
2. E. Boulding *The Underside of History* (Colorado 1976) p. 38.
3. For example, R. Ardrey *The Social Contract* (New York 1970); L. Tiger *Men in Groups* (New York 1971); R. Tiger and J. Shepher *Women in the Kibbutz* (New York 1975).
4. Boulding *The Underside of History* p. 77.
5. *Ibid.* pp. 111-156.
6. *Ibid.* pp. 170-172, 192-193. For the debate over Mother Goddesses see S. Pomeroy *Goddesses, Whores, Wives, and Slaves* (New York 1976) pp. 13-15.
7. Pomeroy *op. cit.* p. 4.
8. Boulding *The Underside of History*, p. 191.
9. *Ibid.* p. 146.
10. C. Safilios-Rothschild 'The Current Status of Women Cross-Culturally' *Theological Studies* 36:4 (Dec. 1975) 577-604. Boulding reports that many legends associate woman with the invention of the alphabet (an ironic bit of evidence of women's analytic-cognitive potential in the light of later patterns of illiteracy and denial of intellectual power). See R. Graves *The White Goddess: A Historical Grammar of Poetic Myth* (New York 1966).
10. See 1 Tim. 2:15.
11. Matt. 19:28.
12. P. Bird 'Images of Women in the Old Testament' in *Religion and Sexism* ed. R. Ruether (New York 1974) p. 77.
13. M. French *The Women's Room* (New York 1978) p. 289.
14. C. C. Gould and M. W. Wartofsky *Women and Philosophy* (New York 1976) p. 192.
15. *Ibid.* p. 263, 23.
16. *Summa Theologica* 1 q. 92, a. 1, ad. lm; *id., Supplementum,* q. 39, a. 1.
17. See Pope John XXIII *Pacem in Terris*, # 41-43 in *The Gospel of Peace and Justice* ed. J. Gremillion (New York 1976) pp. 209-210; *A.A.S.* 55 (20 April 1963) no. 5, 267.
18. Emphasis added. *Gaudium et Spes* # 29, # 60 in *The Documents of Vatican II* ed. W. Abbott (New York 1966) pp. 227-228, 267; *A.A.S.* 58 (7 December 1966) 15, 1048-49, 1080.
19. Pope Paul VI 'Reconciliation—the Way to Peace' *Origins*; *A.A.S.* 67 (31 January 1975) p. 65.
20. Pope Paul VI *Ministeria Quaedam; A.A.S.* 64 (31 August 1972) pp. 8, 533; Sacred Congregation for the Doctrine of the Faith, *Declaration on the Question of the Admission of Women to the Ministerial Priesthood; A.A.S.* 69 (28 February 1977) 115.
21. A. Montagu *The Nature of Human Aggression* (New York 1976) pp. 7-8, 48.
22. See note 3. For critiques of these theories see A. Montagu *op. cit.* pp. 8-22, Boulding *The Underside of History* pp. 35-52.
23. J. Money and P. Tucker *Sexual Signatures on Being a Man or a Woman* (Boston 1975) pp. 37-39.

24. A. Montagu *The Nature of Human Aggression* p. 19.

25. E. Maccoby and C. Jacklin *The Psychology of Sex Differences* (California 1974) pp. 243-247, 360.

26. S. E. Jacobs and K. Hansen *Anthropological Studies of Women* (privately published 1977) p. 57.

27. 1 Cor. 11:3-12, 14:34-35; Eph. 5:22; Col. 3:18; 1 Pet. 3:1 and 1 Tim. 8:15 must be seen within the context of Eph. 5:21, 25, 33 and 1 Cor. 13:7, 3-4; Gal. 3:27-28; 2 Cor. 6:18; Acts 2:17-18. See J. Komonchak 'Theological Questions on the Ordination of Women' in *Women and Catholic Priesthood* ed. A. M. Gardiner (New York 1976) pp. 247-249.

28. Mark 2:27.

29. John 4:5-26; 11:17-37.

30. John 4:28-42; 12:7-8.

31. Luke 10:38-42. It is notable that nothing is known of the sexual status of Martha and Mary.

32. E. Carroll 'The Proper Place for Women in the Church' in Gardiner *Women and Catholic Priesthood* p. 16.

33. *Gaudium et Spes*, # 13, 1034-35.

34. B. Boutreau 'Neo-Feminism and the Next Revolution in Consciousness' *Cross Currents* (New York 1977) XXVII, 170-182.

35. Mark 1:15.

36. Mark 3:31-35.

37. Mark 10:42-45 and parallels.

38. G. Baum *Man Becoming* (New York 1971) at p. 167: When the Church enters a new environment and men ask new salvational questions, the focus of the gospel may change without, however, affecting the self-identity of the gospel. This shift of focus is not a worldly process: . . . The refocusing of the gospel is the work of the Spirit. It is brought about by the Church's fidelity to God's Word addressed to her in the present. Through the memory of Jesus Christ, the Christian community is able to discern God's Word addressing it in history now, and through a process of dialogue and some conflict, involving the whole community and eventually even the hierarchy, the entire Church enters into obedience to the divine Word.

39. F. Morrisey 'Juridical Status of Women' in *Sexism and Church Law* ed. J. Coriden (New York 1977) p. 4.

40. Note the increasing presence of women in the highest elective political offices: Simone Veil as President of the European Parliament; Margaret Thatcher, prime minister of Great Britain; Indira Gandhi's spectacular return to power in India.

41. *Gaudium et Spes* # 44; *A.A.S.* 69 (28 February 1972), 1048-49.

42. Pope Paul VI *Populorum Progressio* # 15; *A.A.S.* 59 (15 April 1967) 4, 265.

Marie Augusta Neal

Pathology of the Men's Church

THE MAIN pathology in a men's Church is that it is a Church for a man's world at a time when there is no longer a need to celebrate such a one-sided world. With the realisation of a base world population of five billion people for the 1980s, with the attendant social crises that characterise that development, we can no longer survive with a division of labour that leaves to men the full responsibility for major economic and political choices. Churches celebrate social systems. The main pathology that characterises a world of five billion people is not its size or the distribution of its people but the fact of the enormous gap between the rich and the poor and the anomaly that enormous wealth, except for Japan's, is concentrated in Christian nations in North America, Western Europe, Australia and New Zealand. The countries to which these nations sent missionaries, traders, and industrialists have developed little more than the export industries in the senders' interests. Local capital is almost non-existent. Prices are unstable. Tariffs discriminate against local manufacturing. There are unfavourable terms of trade, and Western monopoly is in middleman profits. In sum, there is a bias against the interests of poor and colonial peoples.[1] In the poor nations education is still minimal. What education has been developed is what is needed to make a faithful servant people. The gains in export are for the rich trading nations. This disparity is now reaching enormous proportions given the distribution of the population base on which it rests. Furthermore, the disparity is now reaching back into the colonising countries.

If the function of religion were merely to celebrate what we have accomplished in the struggle for existence as some modern scientific humanists proclaim,[2] this might be considered cause for rejoicing since, in the precarious struggle, the Christians may survive while others perish. But from a Christian perspective that achievement is pathological.

53

Following the biblical mandate, we have increased and multiplied and filled the earth. Population size is now a social problem. We cannot rest as on the seventh day with the Lord and proclaim that this is good. To continue to give priority to this mandate to increase, given the base population size, is pathological. As a Church we have already redirected our primary focus to a second gospel task which points up the pathologies that accompany a continuation of the first mandate beyond the point of its fulfilment. The priority, just as richly grounded in Scripture, but not as richly implemented as yet is the mandate to do social justice on the land. This mandate reached full expression after its first eighty years of development from *Rerum Novarum* in 1891 (Leo XIII), through the *Call to Action*, 1971 (Paul VI).[3]

The Church has accepted a very serious social task in aligning itself with the development of peoples and calling its membership to action to realise social justice in the world. This innovation has come after several centuries of primary focus on an otherworldly spirituality which encouraged the membership to so focus attention on final salvation that action in this world, expressing concern for the neighbour's social development was suspect of worldliness. Even the social efforts that were made gave primacy to 'the spiritual works of mercy', reducing 'the corporal works of mercy' to the alleviation of the results of poverty rather than to the elimination of the causes of human misery. The former emphasis on ultimate salvation with attendant indifference to the social consequences of this emphasis is the major cultural source of the pathologies that characterise the male Church today. Scripture insists on planned social action for the achievement of ultimate salvation. It provides directives that demand response to the material needs even of strangers and of enemies.[4] Despite these gospel directives, society has developed under Church auspices with strong family, ethnic and national solidarities wherein racially and ethnically different people are excluded and even left to die as if some other tribal gods were responsible for their lives.

It is not the animal nature of this very natural behaviour that is pathological; it is the Church's condoning of it by celebrating systems that practice it. This linking of the Church goals with societal goals was so manifest by the beginning of the twentieth century that a leading sociologist concluded from observation that the God people worshipped was nothing more than the society which sustained them.[5] For even as the otherwordly emphasis was preached as holy, Church administrators were making financial, organisational and educational decisions in the name of the Church, modelled on wordly business interests. This separation of ends and means is sufficiently noted in *Mater et Magistra*,[6] to allow us to conclude that these pathologies can be characterised as those of the man's

Church if one assumes, and I do, that those who have the power to make the decisions have the obligation to accept responsibility for decisions made.[7]

Basically, the pathologies of the Church are the pathologies of the society. The Church as church, that is as a moral solidarity of people who worship God conceived in specific images and worshipped in a limited range of accepted styles, legitimates behaviour in the political, economic and class structure of society by celebration of liturgy and by affirming prayer styles that help to orient the people to the existing social order.

In the perspective of a century-long Christian Church effort to implement a socially sensitive ethic of justice, we can look at three crises that characterise the men's world and the attendant Church structures that support this world: the arms race, premature production of nuclear energy, and the declining quality of life in patriarchal society.

When the social order provides for the production of arms with a destructive capacity sufficient to destroy the world's population twelve times over, and the Church which affirms life cannot mobilise its members to a social consciousness sufficient to resist furthering that move to world destruction, it is time to look at the basic assumptions on which these attitudes towards war rest as well as at the mentality of the consultants the Church uses for keeping itself informed for making moral decisions.

The division of labour between men designing and producing implements to destroy life, and women concentrating their energies in the production and sustaining of the life of those men, has resulted in our having no academically-taught ethic that can compellingly convince the youth of the world that destruction of human life to resolve economic problems and social differences is a violation of our humanity and a contradiction of our Christian faith. We still affirm ethics that so firmly assume the naturalness of human use of violence that they are sufficiently persuasive to allow for the development of an internationally-sponsored industry in weapons-production larger than a corresponding productive system for food to sustain life. It is a basic pathology to solve problems of life with weapons of death.

At the Faith, Science, and the Future Conference of the World Council of Churches held at Massachusetts Institute of Technology in the summer of 1979, physical scientist Philip Morrison of M.I.T. revealed that our world resources in nuclear weapons have ultimate destructive power. Just considering nuclear weapons of over a megaton of destructive energy each, the United States has 7,000 such weapons, the Soviet Union 4,600, the United Kingdom 200, France 250, China 150, and India, South Africa and Israel a potential for making them. When two nations produce sufficient destructive power in weapons to destroy the entire world population twelve times over and six other nations aspire to do the same, the world system that condones such production is pathological.

Churches constitute moral solidarities that can provide an environment for reflection on such actions towards profound modification and change of such a system. When a Church then, given this reality, focuses its apostolic efforts on psychologically-based pastoral counselling to help people survive within such a system, rather than on the examination and change of the broad social causes of that system, that is pathology.

To remain ambivalent concerning the morality of the production of nuclear energy itself, when concerned scientists have been explicit in explaining the fact that there is as yet no known way of disposing of the nuclear waste which plants produce in daily normal operation, and when administrators continue to make decisions not only to dispose of the waste in non-durable containers when they know that the waste will remain dangerous for thousands of years beyond the natural life of the containers, and that the most serious effect of the waste is its cancer-producing potential when ingested as food or drink, and that the waste will contaminate the ground where the food grows and the streams from which the drinking water will come, that is pathological.

Furthermore, in a world living under the potential danger of nuclear war and hence facing the potential destruction of the most carefully-sealed radioactive waste containers, and, further, when the containers are set near earthquake faults, when plants dispose of their wastes secretly near where deprived populations reside, to assume that the nuclear plants and their secret waste-disposal systems located where defenceless people live will not be subject to destructive acts, is a pathology. Churches that condone such systems by silence, indifference, or culpable ignorance created by the planned omission of such knowledge from the seminary training of male candidates to the ministry, induce pathology. Emphasis on personal holiness and communal solidarity in such a world system of planned destruction cuts God down to tribal size when the idea of God and God's relationship to the universe is all encompassing and the idea of a Catholic Church all inclusive.

When so much evidence demonstrates that in its present form, the world political economy cannot provide adequately for all of the world's population and yet it continues in a form to provide for only one third, failing to provide for the oppressed third to the point of having to will its death, when such a condition exists, and that condition exists now, the Church that continues to affirm human production in ways that exacerbate that problem and fails, at the same time, to provide itself with effective deliberative bodies that can address humane solutions even though it has within its power to do so, that is a pathology. When a Church following the mandates of its own gospel, announces to the world that all are one in the action of the resurrected Saviour and then proceeds to affirm a world structure that provides status and resources to some, drudgery work to others, and deprives a third of the world's people of resources sufficient for mere survival, by preaching celebration of life to the advantaged, moral discipline to the workers, and patient waiting for a heaven to the dispossessed, then those sermons by reason of their affirmation of the unequal distribution of the world's resources in line with the *status quo* which provides only for the survival of advantaged classes, are a serious pathological use of the Word.[8]

At present, hate is institutionalised in war, self-interest in the economy, and love in the family. Science provides major attempts today to legitimate these divisions by calling them natural.[9] The Church can be used to make these divisions seem holy by shaping ideas about God to fit them. When this occurs, the language of the Church has become pathological. There is reason to think it has occurred even though the Church has proclaimed that action on behalf of justice is a constitutive dimension of the gospel.[10] Effective directives to implement that mandate meet resistance from Church administrators. There does exist leverage for change however. This justice mandate is embodied in the Human Rights Covenants of the United Nations[11] to the shaping of which the churches have made a major contribution.[12] These covenants affirm everyone's rights to health care, education, social security, union organising, by reason of being human and not on the basis of mere citizenship. They affirm also the rights of peoples to the use of their lands and land resources; in a word—social rights. These are accompanied by the affirmation of the rights of individuals to fair trial, freedom of speech, assembly and religion, the vote; in a word—to personal freedom as well as social security. These documents preclude the institutionalisation of hate in political struggle and self-interest in the economy, and in turn they call for the extension of love well beyond the family, local community, and nation.

How to redirect these natural and human qualities to just political, economic, and social ends calls for a challenge to the naturalness of class struggle and in turn to a reorganisation of the role relations between men and women in society, because basic to currently institutionalised relationships is the primary emphasis on sexual partnerships. Such partnerships are still essential to life but no longer are the primary model for survival. New models of peer relationships are needed and new skills in acting as peers as well. What is needed is commitment to human solidarity rooted in faith and devoid of secret assumptions about male or white superiority rooted in beliefs about the image of God.[13] The recognition that sin in all its manifestations is social and associated with the giving and taking of life is needed.

We need a radical transition to a new focus for doing God's will, a

E

transition from an ethnic fostering of life to a global development of peoples, an extension of our vision of membership from ethnic solidarity and class ascendency within these narrow limits to a new understanding of the freedom of the people of God, a discovery that altruism is an attainable virtue with God's help.

Our traditional models for the division of labour into heart and head, sky and earth, slave and free; in a word—female and male, black and white, poor and rich, servant and served preclude this expansiveness. The ultimate pathology of these narrow models is the life-boat ethic now formalised as a plausible solution of a too-crowded world.[14] That the scientific community would contemplate such a solution given the alternatives possible with a different world economy is itself the most serious of pathologies. (The immigration limitations of nations of the First and Second Worlds is a current manifestation of this pathology but then so is the basic logic of international finance. The basic assumptions of the international system of production, trade and access to resources needed for survival are rooted in myths of self-interest that prevent the solution of problems of human survival and allow for the development of processes of human destruction of world proportion.) It is not that the problems have no technical solution. It is that the parameters for resolving problems of human life at the present time are too narrow for the variables that need to be included. Our basic myths exclude some people's stories. Our ideas about God and God's relationship with the world are limited to a man's Church in a man's world.[15] The people who assemble to deliberate the world's problems with the power to make decisions do not represent the historical divisions allowed to develop by those who had and still have the power to make those decisions. In order to eliminate pathological uses of power that have caused human oppression, the people who assemble to deliberate and decide must represent all of the people. Before this can happen the Church must recognise that all its members are made in God's image and are called to God's will.[16] The Church must also recognise that the form of its worship is the form of the world, which form it shapes in symbol and ritual. When access to God is constrained by the form, the form is pathological.

Notes

1. Barbara Ward was speaking about this abnormality in the early 1960s. See her *The Rich Nations and the Poor Nations* (New York 1962).
2. Edward O. Wilson *On Human Nature* (Cambridge 1978) pp. 192, 206. In contrast, see Franz Fanon *Black Skins White Masks* (New York 1967) p. 89.
3. Leo XIII, *A.S.S.* 23: 641-670. The Latin text of Paul VI's *Octogesima Adveniens* appears in *L'Osservatore Romano*, 15 May 1971. His *Populorum Progressio*, 21, *A.S.S.* 59 (1967) 257-299 is also a major social justice document. The whole series of documents of the Roman Catholic and Protestant churches that address the question of social justice in the last century are analysed in four issues of *Church Alert*, Nos. 17 through 20, 1977 and 1978, SODEPAX, Geneva.
4. See, for example, Luke 3:10-11; Matt. 25:31-46; Mark 10: 25; Isa. 58:6-8.
5. Emile Durkheim *Les Formes Elementaire de la Vie Religieuse* (Paris 1912).
6. John XXIII, 15 May 1961 in *A.A.S.* 53 (1961) 401-464.
7. Marie Augusta Neal *Values and Interests in Social Change* (New Jersey 1965).
8. Max Weber *Religions–Sociologie* (J. C. B. Mohr, Germany 1922). Chapters VI, VII, VIII.
9. Wilson *On Human Nature*.
10. Roman Synod 'Justice in the World' 1971, paragraph 6.
11. United Nations 'International Covenants on Human Rights and Optional Protocol' United Nations Office of Public Information, November 1976.
12. See Pontifical Commission 'Justita et Pax' *The Church and Human Rights* Working Paper No. 1 (Vatican City 1975) and *Church Alert* The SODEPAX Newsletter, Nos. 17, 18, 19, 20, 1977 and 1978, Ecumenical Centre, Geneva, Switzerland. These issues review the social thinking of the churches from a Catholic and Protestant perspective. See also the more recent documents of the Latin American Bishops Conference (CELAM), Puebla, Mexico 1979 and of the Canadian Conference of Bishops 'Witness to Justice: A Society to Be Transformed' May 1979, Ottawa, Ontario. The Call to Action Conference of the United States Conference of Bishops held in Detroit in 1976 had a similar function.
13. 'The Concept of God in Black Theology' by Sabelo Ntwasa and Basil Moore in *The Challenge of Black Theology in South Africa* ed. Basil Moore (Atlanta, Georgia 1974) pp. 18-28.
14. See Garrett Hardin 'The Tragedy of the Commons' *Science* 162 (1968) 1243-1248 and his 'Living on a Lifeboat' *BioScience* 24 (1974) 561-568.
15. Marie Augusta Neal 'Women in Religious Symbolism and Organization' in *Religious Change and Continuity* ed. Harry M. Johnson, Jossey-Bass (San Francisco 1979) pp. 218-250.
16. See 'Vatican Declaration: Women in the Ministerial Priesthood' *Origins* 33 (3 February 1977) 519-523. See also J. O'faolain and L. Martines (ed.) *Not in God's Image* (New York 1973).

PART III

Theological Perspectives

Rosemary Haughton

Is God Masculine?

1. INTRODUCTION

THE TITLE for this essay is useful in its apparent foolishness, for what
we are talking about is not the nature of God but the way in which human
beings experience the action of God and there is no doubt that most
God-language mediates that experience in terms of a masculine kind of
presence and activity.

For the purposes of this discussion I am using the words 'masculine' and
'feminine' in a descriptive way to refer to the fact that all societies have
some distinction of sexual roles and that appropriate behaviour patterns
develop in the particular social order, so that within wide limits it is
possible to use these adjectives without prejudice and know what we
intend by them.

The attribution of a predominantly masculine character to the deity
was virtually inevitable in a succession of cultures—Hebrew, Greek,
Roman and Roman-derived—which took masculine superiority for
granted. The effect of this is important not just because of the results for
women but because of the inevitable effect of this unconscious basis for
thought on the whole self-awareness of the Church, and on the unspoken
assumptions about 'her' proper nature and activities.

We need, however, to have some clear idea of why certain things are
culturally possible at a given moment in history, otherwise we shall be in
danger of judging the past by the present, or *vice versa*.

Christianity maintains that history has meaning. It is neither a cyclic
recurrence nor a fated sequence, but a kind of dialectical progression
between God and human beings, of gift and response. If history is real,
because people actually choose to love, or not, to obey, or not, then
change is real, and each little change re-creates the situation in which love

is given and received or refused. In individual human lives this is comparatively easy to see, but it applies also to whole cultures and to the human race. But in such vast complexes changes cannot happen all at once but will begin in individuals and small groups, and only gradually become diffused. Often we cannot tell where it began, because history only becomes aware of change when it is already quite widely diffused.

The change with which I am chiefly concerned here is the rise to consciousness of the sense of the feminine in human nature. What we are seeing has never happened before, although signs of it, identifiable by hindsight, were present long ago.

2. PSYCHOLOGICAL REFLECTIONS

It is now a truism of psychology that there is a masculine and a feminine element in all human beings. This 'contrasexual' element has always been present, naturally, but women interpreted their feminine experience in terms of masculine consciousness, since the shape and order of society was necessarily conscious and therefore masculine in character. The feminine was powerful, but its power was unconscious, manifested in symbols (often mediated through goddesses and their cultic practices) of the fertile earth, of the hidden womb from which all life comes, of night and death which dissolve all shape and distinctness, of the untameable power of sexuality which drives sensible people mad. All the mysterious and elusive aspects of life belonged to the domain of the feminine, and its power was feared, and that fear was articulated in attitudes to actual women, rationalised in terms of the natural inferiority of women, who were dangerous because morally essentially unstable and in need of masculine protection and direction.

In societies in which these mechanisms operated the result was a religious interpretation which could help to cope with the immense power of the feminine by keeping the symbols, and their human 'carriers', separate. Such religious articulated their myth, ritual and external organisation in terms of the masculine aspect, which lives in daylight and can plot cause and effect and make decisions on that basis, creating a religious society to fit the needs of the people. This was, while the feminine was 'unconscious', the *only way religion could develop at all*, as a sane articulation of the deepest and mysterious realities. When, occasionally, the unconscious, feminine powers did revolt, as in the Dionysian cults and some mediaeval sects, the result easily became destructive, because the feminine was operating unmediated out of the unconscious, not balanced by reason and conscious reflection. The unpleasant results of masculine-dominated religion are simply the side-effects of the need to make available to human beings, in a form they could live with, the terrifying experience of the God who is their deepest being.

The masculine God-language was culturally necessary, and the false assumptions and injustices that sprang from it were, in a sinful world, inevitable. Though the Spirit is our very being, yet in our state of refusal we cannot bear that vision. But God's desire for the love of human beings is not lessened by refusal, it comes to us where the resistance is least, which is often in our consciousness of beauty, of strangeness, of need. God does not force upon those depths, because that would simply destroy. Rather, human response to the awareness of God worked to create a ritual, protected, place of encounter. So ritual and social and moral experience were articulated in ways felt to be appropriate to the Presence known in the mysterious encounter. Individuals, protected by the law and the common life of a God-directed people, could come to know the Lord, and mysterious, irrational religious experience could be contained *within* the system, by being articulated in the cults of gooddesses.

3. THE OLD TESTAMENT

The Hebrew religion was explicitly monotheist. All the ritual and moral detail, all prayer and hope, was directed to the service of the One God and there was therefore no possibility of mediating the feminine through symbols of goddesses. What could happen to the kind of experience of God which, in other religions, could be attributed to goddesses?

As long as the Hebrew people were in process of fighting for survival, conquering and settling, the masculine type of religious culture suited them very well, as we see in the 'historical' books, because all those things require a masculine type of awareness. When the people became more settled and less concerned with external decision-making, they began to 'go after foreign gods', which meant the darkly powerful goddesses of fertility. In response to this, the prophets began to develop a theology in which God emerges with a different kind of 'personality'. The God of Isaiah, and Hosea, and of Job, is a very different kind of person from the 'historical' God of Moses. He is altogether more unpredictable, mysterious, strange and compassionate, but often as apparently arbitrary and wayward as any female.

Finally there emerged a feminine 'description' of the divine within the theology of the one God. This was the theology, with its underlying human psychology, which was adopted by Paul, and the writer to the Hebrews, as appropriate for the definition of the meaning of Jesus, and was for John a language for the articulation of his personal experience of Jesus.

In absorbing the 'Wisdom' style of contemporary literature, the religion of Israel modified the cynical and pessimistic outlook of the sages, expressing it within a religious consciousness in which God is shaper of the people's history for his own saving purposes. Unable to content herself with pithy maxims for getting through life more or less successfully, Wisdom was forced to break out in search of a self-expression more adequate to Israel's rich awareness of her God. The Wisdom writings, though they span several hundred years, all echo the same startling consciousness that Wisdom is not merely God's gift to humankind, but is identified with him in power and function in creation, in the guidance of individuals, and in the history of God's people. Some important passages (from the Deutero-canonical books with the exception of Proverbs) are: Proverbs 8:22-9:6; Wisdom 7:21-9:11 (also, as illustrating the point made, long accounts of the activity of Wisdom in history); Sirach 1:1-20, 24:1-22. There are others, e.g., in Job, Baruch, and some psalms.

The theology of Wisdom is about the divine nature as known and working in human life. In some places Wisdom is identified with 'knowledge' and with 'the Law', and in others 'the Spirit' of God is described in terms used to describe Wisdom. In both cases it refers to a knowledge and observance of Law which relates people immediately to God by working *in* them. The divine nature and activity as it is developed under the title of Wisdom is God as a power *within* creation, never 'dissolved' in it, but receiving, and living by, and giving back, the very being of God.

What is being described is a 'feminine' type of presence and activity. It is useful to compare the account of creation in the first chapters of Genesis, with the description of the activity of Wisdom in creation (in 'Wisdom' 7 and 8). In the former, God forms and 'places' created things. We watch him making the world. He views it *from without*, and is satisfied. This is a masculine image of conscious, visible, reasonable planning. In the Wisdom passages we see 'creation from within' a continuous process of 'ordering', shaping, inspiring, sustaining, changing. It is equally the work of 'omnipotence' but it works *within* the situation, and can only be properly grasped by one who, himself, 'lives with Wisdom'.

This development of the sense of God's activity *within* creation, continuously present and shaping it, gives sharper point to Israel's sense of historical meaning. In doing so, it reaches a stage at which, by the inner necessity of her being, the divine nature must somehow become explicit and be communicated in the created mode which she informs and 'orders'. She must 'take root', have a place and a 'home'. This is developed in Chapter 24 of Ben Sirach in a passage which has been fittingly applied to the mother of Jesus, since this is a description of how God is, as it were, 'under the necessity' of *becoming incarnate*.

This is why the images of Wisdom came naturally to Paul when he wanted language to describe the eternal being of the Son who is Jesus and why John found in it the only possible language in which to convey his sense of the sheer intimacy of God's loving relationship with the people in whom he 'became flesh'.

4. THE NEW TESTAMENT

The feminine imagery of divine Wisdom also defines the reality of the male human being, Jesus of Nazareth. Solomon, the sage, is the archetype of the man who 'lives with Wisdom' but 'a greater than Solomon is here'. His masculine qualities—his natural authority, his gift for organisation, his grasp of situations and his powers of debate—are all used in what one might call a 'Wisdom' way so that what is most striking is his swift insight, his ruthless immediacy, his ability to identify with the feelings of others, his integrated awareness which issues in a mastery of symbolic speech, and his power to evoke headlong devotion. He worked, that is, 'from within' as well as seeing and acting decisively 'from without'.

But in the person of Jesus we see the feminine as *conscious*. He had no need to 'suppress' the feminine side of himself, and *therefore* no need to project it onto actual women. He treated them as people—a culturally unprecedented thing to do.

The theological implication of this is that the transforming power of the risen life which is in his Body, the Church, must be striving to re-create this same fullness of human nature *consciously*. Paul said that in Christ there is 'neither male nor female' because what the risen Jesus did was to make available, simply as love, the being of God which, in earthly life, is experienced in the complementary modes imaged in the 'masculine' and 'feminine' ways of experiencing reality.

In the young Church this new awareness briefly over-rode cultural conditioning, and the roles and attitudes of Christian women reflected this. But nobody is *wholly* 'in Christ' in this life. The new consciousness was real but in this particular area there was no way anyone could perceive consciously, and explain, what was going on. As the early illumination dimmed the old way of dealing with the feminine, by separating its power from actual women by putting it into 'myth' prevailed in the Church. We can see that the suppression of the feminine was an 'unnatural' thing to do by the sheer virulence of the anti-feminine rationalisations of many Christian teachers. The language is altogether disproportionate and obsessive.

5. THE HISTORY

To compress a long and complex history, what happened next was that the 'feminine' activity and being of God, the 'Wisdom' kind, which was essential to its health, made itself available to the Church in another way. In proportion as women lost status and so were made incapable of mediating Wisdom to the Church, so the cult of Mary grew, and symbolically made that Wisdom available, even though the cult grew so important that it became suspect. But the Reformation stopped up that entrance, throughout Protestant countries, and the Catholic world allowed itself increasingly to trivialise the great Mother of God into a source of private comfort for the devotee.

The suppressed feminine, denied outlets, forced some. One was the Romantic revival, in which emotions and aspirations outlawed by Reason and Enlightenment gradually became a major cultural influence, thus releasing the feminine into a desiccated culture, but in a 'mysterious', undisciplined and 'dark' form. The other was the feminist movement, when a changing feminine self-consciousness was brought about by, as well as promoting, political struggle for voting and legal rights. Politics was its 'language' since it had to be a *conscious* language (i.e., a masculine one) if it were to be used effectively in a masculine-type culture. Later, the new sense of self-made possible in women—and indirectly in men—by political emancipation demanded deeper self-discovery, and this has been the job of the contemporary 'women's movement'.

6. THE CHURCH

The very life of the Church is the life of Incarnate Wisdom, but because of the exclusively masculine type of power structure in the Church, with its innate conservatism and its underlying anti-feminine phobias, the Church was among the sections of society most resistant to the new awareness. But the Church still had its 'weak spot' in the form of the cult of Mary, enfeebled and sentimentalised though it was, and here divine love touched his Church.

For, by a beautiful paradox of the divine sense of humour, it was in the wholly masculine-dominated Catholic Church that the deep change in human consciousness actually reached definition in the proclamation of the dogma of the Assumption of Mary in 1950. (The date is significant. War, with the social and psychic upheavals it causes, 'loosens' entrenched attitudes and tends to 'let out' carefully hidden forces. The war against Hitler loosened every conceivable psychic structure in the West.)

It was the Swiss Protestant psychologist, Carl Jung, who realised the importance of this event, but even he did not realise its full implications, since his sense of incarnation was deficient. He perceived that the great goddess of the unconscious had been lifted out into the daylight of consciousness and there acclaimed, but beyond that she had been defined as *being bodily in heaven*. Since Mary is not only symbol, but also a real, human woman, to see Mary, crowned and glorious, at the heart of the Trinity, was to see *women* in a new light.

Symbols work whether we are aware or not, and history is irreversible. However, we explain it, from that time the forces for change in the Church, until then suppressed, began to break out, and ten years later a new Pope, old enough and humble enough to listen to Wisdom, 'opened a window'. In through that window came a gale of the Spirit, who is the breath of divine Wisdom herself.

But those who tried to articulate the new insights did so in very masculine terms. Not only were they all men, but they were all the product of an education designed to suppress the feminine element. That it did not entirely succeed is the work of Wisdom indeed, and a proof of the presence of the Spirit in the Church. A new spirit was at work and although this was experienced in terms of a theology still using an exclusively masculine God-language, there are signs of strain, because it was being stretched to accommodate intuitions which were quite beyond its scope.

The result of this 'masculine' approach to renewal has been to highlight those issues in the area of changing attitudes to women and the feminine which could easily be identified in terms of the masculine type of awareness, for instance questions of 'sexist' language in scripture and liturgy, of women in liturgical and ministerial functions, and of the need for changes in the education of priests and religious which would make for better relations between the sexes. Changes have indeed resulted, but these are really only symptoms of a much bigger change, which has been noticed by few because it was not describable in terms of the available language of ecclesiology.

7. CONCLUSIONS

Finally, then, the answer to the question 'Is God masculine?' must be sought in an ecclesial context because it is not a description of God but a description of the Church. The answer must be, 'He was, but is no longer' because of the unprecedented changes in and to the Church now.

All over the world, but especially in the 'Third World', the real vitality of the Body of Christ is now apparent in small groups of Christians without official position or organisation, who come together to help each other in their desire to serve God by prayer and in service of the world, on the model of Jesus himself. These groups include some, even, who have not reached the point of recognising who has drawn them together, but whose lives of service and love and whose deep truthfulness and sincerity show them to be under the guidance of the Spirit. In, and among, all these groups, official and unofficial ministries work together to serve, and celebrate. These little local 'churches' are truly and visibly the Body of Christ. Here Christ is lived, draws people to himself, changes, liberates (politically and spiritually, as *one* freedom) and heals. In Latin America, the C.E.L.A.M. meeting at Puebla endorsed and upheld the *primary* importance of these '*communidages de base*', but they exist everywhere, though often unaware of each other's existence, and almost always quite unaware that they are, indeed, the 'new' Church, emerging not by planning (however, necessary plans may be) but unexpectedly, as is the Lord's way always. They emerge among the poor, the 'marginal' people, the ordinary ones. And the clergy see this, and—increasingly—want to serve these little churches, not by dominating them but simply by being available in and to them in their work of being Christ.

Such a Church is a 'wisdom' type of creation. It requires proper and enlightened organisation. It needs reason and decision—creation 'from without'. But its deepest nature manifests God as Wisdom, working from *within* the world and emerging from it, 'rooted' in particular local situations, 'incarnate' in particular networks of loving relationship. This is an unprecedented change in the very being of the Church, yet it is really only the coming to consciousness of that which was its essential life from the moment of the Resurrection. To recognise it and respond to it requires a degree of heroic humility which comes hard to a masculine and dominating ecclesiastical ethos.

The death to the old, in order that the new may be born from it, is always hard, but it is now required of us. What its practical results will be we can only begin to glimpse. We can see some obvious ones in the 'new' church of the poor, for instance in the changed status of Christian women and in the challenge implied to traditional roles, but the deeper changes will take time. The shift is not from a masculine to a feminine type of ecclesial presence, but from a one-sided Church culture to one which may 'marry' masculine and feminine in a Church which lives from within, outwards, but which uses its God-given 'masculine' awareness to discern and support what emerges, thus bringing forth into the world the full power of the Spirit of Christ, who is the Word and Wisdom of God.

And when someone asks 'Is God masculine?' we shall look at the Church which is his Body, and answer 'God is neither masculine nor feminine; God is love'.

Marie de Merode de Croy

The Role of Woman
in the Old Testament

1. INTRODUCTION

WOMEN COMPLAIN that they have no voice in the Catholic Church
or, more precisely, that they have no official role in it, and that they do not
share in the making of the decisions which direct its future or in the acts by
which it accomplishes its mission. The Church may well be the Body of
Christ before it is anything else, as the Conciliar Constitution *Lumen
Gentium* reminds us (§ 8), but over and above having this spiritual and
divine aspect it also makes up a visible complex, a hierarchic society,
governed or 'animated', as the modern term has it, by ministers whose
essential function is to teach and to sanctify its members, and it is from
this function that women are excluded simply and solely on account of
their sex, and this is why it is sometimes difficult for them to feel that they
are full members of the Church.

Now according to the most recent document of the Holy See on this
matter, the *Declaration on the Question of the Admission of Women to the
Ministerial Priesthood (Inter insigniores)*, this exclusion of women is
based on two essential arguments: (1) the example of Christ who did not
entrust the office of apostles to women even though in his own attitude to
women he was well ahead of his time in the Jewish world revealed above
all in the Old Testament (§ 2); (2) the fact that Christ himself was a man
and that the priest would not be fulfilling his role as a sign and sacrament
of Christ if he were a woman (§ 5). In this connection, the document of the
Holy See cites a few Old Testament texts in support of this thesis or rather
'in harmony with' it. These texts present the covenant of God with his
people in terms of a marriage in which God is the bridegroom and his

71

people is the bride. These texts are picked up by the New Testament and applied to the relationship of Christ with his Church.

It is, therefore, clear that the Old Testament plays an important part in the way in which the Church sees the woman's role today. At the same time we have to admit that these two principal arguments drawn from the Scriptures are for the most part arguments from silence and they are as such difficult to handle, as the Declaration virtually admits when it recognises that they do not 'make the matter immediately obvious' but that they do constitute 'a number of convergent indications' (§ 2).

I do not dispute that it is in the last resort for the Church to discern 'what can change and what must remain immutable' (§ 4). All I should like to do here is to offer a few reflections, as a woman theologian, about the way the Declaration has *used* the Old Testament evidence in connection with these two main arguments.

The Roman document itself acknowledges that it is difficult to discern in the scriptural texts any particular theology of woman, or any particular conception of woman as such on the part of God or of her place in the design of God. The Old Testament does, however, help us to understand indirectly the context of the life Jesus led, the background of his activity, and the sorts of things he was opposing when he did break with the attitude of his time without, however, going so far as to include any women among the Twelve. This is what we shall deal with in Part 2. After that, we shall examine the way in which certain sacred writers were reacting against the attitudes of their contemporaries towards women even in Old Testament times. We shall conclude by looking at the symbolism of marriage in the Old Testament.

2. THE BACKGROUND OF THE OLD TESTAMENT AND THE ATTITUDE OF JESUS

Most of the texts of the Old Testament which mention women present them in their ordinary capacities as wife, mother or mistress of the house. The sacred writers do not stint their praises or their acknowledgment of the importance of women in these roles, starting with the conjugal role in the *Song of Songs*. The conjugal love of Isaac, Jacob, Elcanah, father of Samuel, and of Tobias comes in for particular attention in the books of the Bible, whereas the love of Rebeccas, Rachel, Anna, mother of Samuel, or of Sarah is not emphasised and is seen rather as a woman's natural attitude. 'He who finds a wife finds a good thing', we read in Prov. 18:22; 'be infatuated always with her love', adds Prov. 5:19. But 'a woman will accept any man' (Ecclus. 36:21). The essential feminine qualities are reserve, modesty (26:13-18), kindness (26:23). In the same way, the maternal role is prized from very ancient times: 'Honour your father and your mother', commands the dealogue.[1] Finally, the wisdom literature sings the praises of a beautiful wife 'in her well-ordered house' (Ecclus. 26:16), 'who is not afraid of snow for her household. . . . She makes herself coverings' (Prov. 31:21-22).

To sum up, the Old Testament does not hesitate to praise women in their traditional roles or, correlatively, to berate those who do not live up to these roles: women who are too beautiful (Ecclus. 9:1-9), headstrong or, as we should say, provocative (26:10), wicked, domineering, garrulous and therefore idle (25:13-26), jealous (26:6) or given to drink (26:8). And finally there is concern for fathers on account of their 'daughters', just like that (42:9-11). And the author even writes: 'Better is the wickedness of a man than a woman who does good' (42:14), and 'If she does not do as you direct, separate her from yourself' (25:26; Esther 1:17).

And it is the case that in the context of marriage the Old Testament legislates much more harshly for the woman than for the man. The woman is one of her husband's chattels along with his house (and even after his house, according to Exod. 20:17). Her husband can repudiate her whereas she cannot petition for divorce. The misconduct of a wife is reprimanded much more severely than that of a husband. In other words, the woman is treated like a 'perpetual minor'.[2]

By the time of Jesus the position of the woman had, if anything, got worse. Repudiation of a woman in the case of adultery or even of sterility after ten years was deemed to be a duty. Certain rabbis thought that one could put away one's wife if she 'had burned a dish or if one had found somebody else more beautiful'.[3]

Most of the laws of the Old Testament and of Judaism are about women in the framework of marriage and see women essentially as wives, mothers, mistresses of the household. These laws are for the most part made in order to protect the husband,[4] although also, no doubt, more largely to protect the family and ensure legitimate heirs, to whom the promise that conditioned the existence of Israel could be passed on. It is also within this context, it would seem, that we have to see the rabbinic prescriptions preventing all women, even non-married women, from studying the Scripture (called the Law), which was tantamount to preventing them from studying at all, on the ground that this could divert them from that maternal role which was so binding at the time.[5] Women could go to the synagogue, but, since they did not know the law well, they could not do the reading.

This prohibition on the study of the law will have incalculable consequences on the way women are seen at the dawn of Christianity: since they do not know all the subtleties of the law which had since Esdras in the fifth century become so important in Israel, the woman is not bound to the punctilious observance of all the positive precepts, any more than are

F

slaves and children. And since a woman is not bound to the perfect observance of the law which seals the covenant, some texts go so far as to say that the covenant does not apply to her. This is how an ancient Jewish prayer (dating, at the very latest, from the first century after Jesus Christ) which is preserved in three rabbinic works can be rendered as follows: 'Blessed be God who has not made me a gentile. Blessed be God who has not made me a woman. Blessed be God who has not made me a slave.' So far as the woman is concerned, the reason is that she is not bound to the observance of the commandments. The context and deepest sense of the prayer is the joy of observing the commandments. Nevertheless the assimilation of women to slaves and pagans reveals the esteem in which women were held at the time.

The law was, of course, full of ritual prescriptions which women were not able to fulfil perfectly on account of their frequent contact with blood. This is no doubt the reason why they had a special enclave reserved to them in the temple, between that for the men and that for the gentiles.[6]

Given all this, Jesus' attitude stands out in even greater relief as being quite extraordinary: he teaches women without caring about his disciples' reactions (John 4:27), heals them, sends them out to witness to the resurrection, takes no account of the ritual impurity of the woman with the issue of blood, suggests that a woman's adultery does not merit greater severity (John 8:11), refuses men the right to divorce to the point where the disciples, inured as they are to great laxity in this regard, come out with the completely disillusioned reflection: 'If such is the case of a man with his wife, it is not expedient to marry' (Matt. 19:10). More profoundly, Jesus judges women according to their faith, and not in the first place on account of their ability to fulfil their role as wife, mother or mistress of the household.[7]

This evidence about the institutions of the Old Testament that concern women and the context of the way in which women were regarded in the Old Testament, a context which emerges as being essentially conjugal, maternal and domestic, should not, however, make us lose sight of the exceptional destiny of certain heroines of the Old Testament who were called out of all this traditional setting on a mission. It also looks as if there were more such heroines at the beginning of Israel's history than at the end, after the exile, when the law, and especially laws of ritual purity, took on an ever-growing importance. In this regard, we can take as our point of reference Jeremiah's statement: 'The law shall not perish from the priest, nor counsel from the wise, nor the word from the prophet' (18:18). We can assume that the three categories of spiritual leaders in Israel are being enumerated here.[8] Now, on this basis, we may not find any women priests mentioned in the Old Testament, but we do find wise women and prophetesses.

Wise women are illustrated by the women called to the court in 2 Sam. 14:1-21 and 20:14-22. Prophetesses were typified by Miriam, sister of Moses, Deborah (Judges 4:4-5), Huldah (2 Kings 22:14-22). We should also recall that the prophet Joel announced the coming of the spirit on all flesh: 'Your sons and your daughters shall prophesy. . . . Even upon your manservants and maidservants in those days, I will pour out my spirit' (2:28-29). The way in which Joel emphasises 'even menservants and maidservants', women as well as men, and 'all flesh, your sons and your daughters' suggests that the author is trying, like Jesus after him, to combat the condition imposed upon women and slaves in his own time. This aim comes out more clearly in the accounts of creation and of the fall, which we are, therefore, now going to study.

3. THE ACCOUNT OF THE CREATION

The story of the creation of the human couple is told twice in the Bible. The first account in Genesis 1:27-31, belongs to the priestly tradition, P (about the sixth century). The second, in Genesis 2:18-25, which is the one with which we shall begin, is more ancient (about the ninth century) and belongs to the Jahwist tradition, J, along with the account of the fall in Chapter 3. This account of the fall ends with the announcement of punishments which are the consequence of sin. The author is quite clearly seeking to respond to eternal questions about the human condition: Why does man die? Why does man work with pain and woman give birth with suffering? Why does man dominate the woman? (Genesis 3:16-19). And the author attributes these pains of the human condition to sin. It is very important to realise that these sufferings have not been willed by God and do not belong to the order of creation described in Chapter 2. On the contrary, they represent a frustration and a change of the initial design of God as expressed in the story of the creation in Chapter 2.

The order of creation and the order of sin are, therefore, diametrically opposed. This is why in Chapter 2 we see God creating women as a helper who would correspond to man, literally somebody who would 'face him', in whom he would find a response. Man had found no response in any of the animals which God had brought him, and this is why God created women: 'It is not good that the man should be alone' (Gen. 2:18). The man recognises one of his own kind in the woman, this is the sense of the exclamation in v. 23: 'This at last is bone of my bone and flesh of my flesh' (and see Gen. 29:14). This union, this solidarity, this correspondence of man and woman which is the real point of the story of the creation, is expressed in several ways: the man gives the woman a name derived from his own; the man then leaves behind his father and mother in order to cleave to his wife because the conjugal union goes beyond the tribal union; and finally woman is drawn from Adam's side whereas the animals are modelled from the clay of the earth.

The fact that creation and the fall are diametrically opposed to each other is recognised by most modern commentators. It has, however, not always been like this. We need go no further than the Pauline corpus to see that the author of 1 Tim. 2:11-15, so far from deploring the domination of woman by man, as the author of Genesis 3 does, advocates the submission of the wife on account not merely of sin in general but of *her* sin in particular, whereas Adam 'was not deceived'! We should note that the story in Genesis 3 had never exonerated Adam. On the contrary, Adam's attempt to throw responsibility onto Eve (Gen. 3:12) in no way exonerates him. What is more, the author of 1 Timothy confuses these stages of creation and of sin when he attributes man's authority over woman to the creation itself—'Adam was formed first, then Eve'—for this represents a profound misunderstanding of Genesis 2. The same argument recurs in 1 Cor. 11:3-10. Focusing on certain details of the story, such as the creation of woman out of man, and after and for him, led Paul virtually to fail to respect the context and main thrust of Genesis 2.

This selective manner of arguing on the basis of certain details of the story in order to overwhelm the woman is typical of Jewish thinking expressed in the pseudepigrapha of the last centuries before Jesus Christ and also of rabbinic thought, including that which is documented for New Testament times. Until then the story of the creation of woman was habitually interpreted, when it was noticed at all, on the basis of the radical separation between these two stages of creation and sin. The first account of the creation comes to mind: 'So God created man in his own image, . . . male and female he created them' (Gen. 1:27). This creation in the image of God expresses itself in the fact that both share without distinction in the creative power of God (see v. 28).[9]

Parallel to this, however, and especially in the two centuries before Jesus Christ, another tendency emerges. This grows stronger and stronger and the import of it is to attribute sole responsibility for sin to the woman, whilst Adam is represented as having acted only in order to please his wife. It is in the wake of this tendency that the interpretation of Genesis 3 is then projected onto the account of creation in Genesis 2, in such a way as to make it look as if there are certain signs of woman's inferiority and a justification for her subjection there.[10] This marked tendency should, no doubt, be understood against the backdrop of the exaltation of the law from the time of Esdras onwards, and especially the laws of purity. Women are excluded from the practice and study of the law that was all-important at that time on account of their frequent impurity and in order better to safeguard their maternal role. And ideological and scriptural justification of this exclusion is then sought in the sacred texts themselves. It is this interpretation current at the time of Christ which is taken up by Paul. And this is the way in which it became possible to introduce ideas completely alien and even opposed to the intention of the account of Genesis which had always clearly distinguished the stage of creation or God's initial design and the stage of sin which thwarted this initial design.

What we should, however, note, in the case of the author of Genesis and in that of Jesus alike, is that they both distinctly and deliberately distanced themselves from the attitudes towards women which prevailed in their respective times. Women lived under a male domination which Jesus attributed to the 'hardness of hearts' on the occasion of that teaching of his on divorce which seeks to return beyond the Mosaic law to 'the beginning', to re-establish the stage of creation, to rediscover the initial design of God, to restore it.

4. THE NUPTIAL SYMBOLISM

Everything I have said so far about Jesus' courageous reaction against the customs of his time is acknowledged by the Roman Declaration, which does, however, also go on to ask why Jesus did not take the further step of himself calling women to the apostolic ministry. This is the final point I wish to examine.

The Declaration attaches great importance to the fact the priest represents a sign of the *man* Jesus, a sign which it says is 'in harmony' with the scriptures that present the covenant under the image of a marriage in which God, then Christ, is the bridegroom and the people, then the Church, is the bride.

This may be so, but we may ask whether it is legitimate to draw any normative conclusions about the respective roles of husband and wife from the image of conjugal love applied to the covenant. The woman represented the people of God at the time when this image was applied to the covenant because her role was thought of as passive in the culture of the period. The husband can represent God or Christ in so far as the husband has authority and initiative in the conjugal relationship and the priest is correspondingly thought of as a man. But in so far as these roles are regarded in a different light, as they are today, I wonder whether it is always 'significant' to think of God as a husband and of the priest, sacrament of Christ, as a man. Is it true that the incarnation of the Word according to the male sex 'cannot be dissociated from the economy of salvation'? Put in another way, does the economy of salvation demand, of itself, and in every culture, that Christ be a man?

5. CALLING WOMEN TO THE MINISTRY?

So far, then, I have expressed certain reflections on the second scriptural argument of the Roman document. Before concluding, let us return to the first argument. The Declaration acknowledges that Christ's attitude towards women was in sharp contrast to that of his Jewish contemporaries, but it makes use of this observation to conclude that it is all the more surprising and significant that Jesus did not in fact call women to the apostolic ministry. We should, however, note that neither did Christ call pagans, which has not prevented the Church from doing so. Jesus and Paul had to observe a certain order of priorities. Paul thought it was essential that pagans should be able to enter the Church as full members, whereas he did not think that a betterment of women's condition was essential, especially in the apocalyptic climate of the beginnings of Christianity (see 1 Cor. 7).

What we are dealing with here, however, is an argument from silence which is difficult to handle, as I said at the beginning. Thus the document goes on by insisting (§ 6) on the fact that the Church is not a human society and should not model its attitude on that of modern democracies in which women in principle have access to the same responsibilities as men. I should in this regard like to pose the question: Should the Church not be trying to integrate the values of liberty which it recognises and appreciates in modern democracies into the human aspect of the Church, that complex visible to the eyes which I mentioned at the beginning?

The document finally asserts that the 'priestly office cannot become the goal of social advancement' for 'it is of another order' (§ 6). Here too we can pose a question: Has the priesthood itself not got an aspect 'visible to the eyes' and is it not a good thing that it should be lived and wanted as a positive thing even humanly speaking, in other words, in effect as a sort of human advancement? Is it not a pity that the Church should keep away from the priesthood beings for whom it is endowed with such value? Is the profound meaning of the incarnation not that the human being should be judged worthy to reveal God and that human values should be taken up into God?

6. CONCLUSION

A study of the Old Testament evidence about women in the light of the Roman document has allowed us to review the texts which the Church uses today when it considers the role of women.

The Church criticises the by and large negative attitude of Judaism and it acknowledges that Christ went beyond this, but only up to a certain point, because, in the final analysis, the fact that Christ called men, and exclusively men, in a way that is rooted in the Old Testament, is said to be something that 'cannot be dissociated from the economy of salvation' and it is not seen as a cultural fact independent of the content of the revealed message in the way, for instance, that considerations about the ritual impurity of women are.

In the same way, the images which present the relationship of God with his people under the aspect of marriage are also declared to belong to the content of the revealed message, contrary, for example, to the image of a treaty between suzerain and vassal, which is another way in which the relationship of God and his people is often represented in the Old Testament.

I thought it was important to reflect on the way in which the Church makes use of the revealed message when it elaborates its teaching on the role of women.

Translated by Iain McGonagle

Notes

1. Exod. 20:12. For other references and concrete examples, see my article in *La Foi et le temps* (1975) 118-119.

2. R. de Veux *Les Institutions de l'Ancien Testament* (Paris 1958) I pp. 48, 60-62, 67-69.

3. J. Bonsirven *Le Judaisme palestinien au temps de Jésus Christ* (Paris 1935) II pp. 107, 207, 211-214.

4. With the exception of Deut. 21:10-14; Exod. 21:7-11; Deut. 24:17.

5. See *Rev. Theol. Louv.* (1978) 181-183 for further details about the matters dealt with in the following paragraphs.

6. Flavius Josephus *Contra Apion* II, p. 8.

7. *La Foi et le temps* pp. 125-128, and, in regard to Paul, at p. 129.

8. In the Judaic epoch, the priest as it were absorbed the functions of wise man and prophet in so far as he taught the law, the unique centre of religion in Israel. This is why the wise women and prophetesses disappeared. See *La Foi et le temps* pp. 123-124.

9. See also Tob. 8:6 and Ecclus. 36:26 (24).

10. For further details, see *Rev. Theol. Louv.* (1977) 338-345.

René Laurentin

Jesus and Women:
An Underestimated Revolution

DID CHRIST initiate a revolution in favour of women? Despite the
extremist attitudes of certain feminist movements which have issued a
global condemnation of the 'male chauvinism' of Christianity, the most
enlightened feminists, those who do honour to the women's struggle of
our time, are beginning to recognise the existence of positive elements for
a reply to that question.[1] Without wishing to enter into the polemics
concerning the extremist slogans of a certain kind of male anti-feminism,
and of female anti-masculinism, and without disparaging the eloquence
which is appropriate to militant liberation movements, we are here concerned to show, positively and succinctly, *whether* and *in what respects*
Jesus adopted innovatory and liberating attitudes towards women.

1. A CHRISTIAN REVOLUTION: THE COMMON SIGN OF INITIATION FOR MEN AND WOMEN

We shall take as our point of departure an immensely important fact,
attested as a development flowing from the teaching of Jesus in the
gospels. In Christianity, the initiation rite, baptism, was conferred on
men and women alike, without any restriction and without any apparent
hesitation (Acts 8:12).

This fact runs counter to the tradition of Judaism, in which the initiation rite was exclusively masculine: circumcision. Must one attribute
to divine revelation the fact that the peoples of the Bible did not adopt
female circumcision,[2] that mutilating rite which is and was widespread in
so many civilisations? At all events, the introduction of a rite which was
no longer masculine, nor sexually-oriented, but broadly human, estab-

80

lished the new community on a new basis which was less particular, more universal, and which transcended sexual divisions. This fact is of incalculable significance. Rituals normally have more practical influence than ideological declarations.[3]

In Judaism, women did not belong to the liturgical community (thus we find the expression: 'to say nothing of women and children' (Exod. 12:37, Deut. 3:19 etc., echoed by the most male-oriented of the gospels: Matt. 14:21, and 15:38), nor to the *royal priesthood* of all men (Exod. 19:6)).[4]

Even today, except in certain liberal synagogues, women have a marginal status, in some side-aisle or gallery. They are not obliged to take part in the act of worship. They attend if their household duties allow them enough leisure. Man is the mediator of the woman: a situation abolished by the extension of the royal priesthood to men and women, according to the New Testament (1 Pet. 2:9).

The first Christian gathering, that of Pentecost, includes men and women (Acts 1:14-15) who all receive the baptism of the Spirit and the charisma (Acts 1-2). If Paul sets limits to the activity of women in Church meetings, he recognises women's right to prophesy, already evident in the Old Testament (*supra* note 4). Despite his reputation as an anti-feminist, this apostle is the very man who was responsible for the most lapidary formulation of the Christian revolution: 'There is neither male nor female' (Gal. 3:28).

The innovatory quality of Christianity's common initiation-rite for everyone is all the more striking in that the baptism of John seems to have been accorded only to the male sex: at least, those mentioned by the Gospels belong exclusively to that category (Luke 3:12-14; see Matt. 3:7-10; John 1:19, 35, etc.).[5]

This revolution in ritual was established without controversy or dispute, and without any formal precept having been preserved for us. Even the text of Matthew—the only one which explicitly states the baptismal formula: 'Baptise all nations in the name of the Father and of the Son and of the Holy Spirit' (Matt. 28:19)—does not spell out the fact that women must be baptised as well as men. The fact was so self-evident that it compelled recognition. It emerged, not from a text, but from an inspiration and a praxis which obviously originate with Jesus himself. What then were his attitude and his impact on the situation?

2. THE INNOVATION AND SHOCKING ATTITUDE OF JESUS

Jesus, who has not left us any formal teaching concerning women, displayed an attitude towards them which was new enough to shock even his disciples (John 4:27). It was probably through their concern to serve his memory that they did not stress the embarrassing elements it contained for what was then 'modern man'. So much had to be done to compel recognition of the glory of Jesus in face of objections from so many mortal enemies that they had to choose the points on which to fight, to gain acceptance of the essential without provoking, on the subject of women, the kind of irresistible outcry which was so familiar to the preachers of the gospel, such as the apostle Paul at Athens (Acts 17:32-34).

2.1. *Common elements in the four gospels*

The fundamental fact of the gospel is that women form part of the community of the kingdom called into existence by Jesus. This community is not masculine, as was that of the rabbis. Its women members are not accidental beneficiaries of the miracles of Jesus. The gospels even tend to point to them rather as privileged beneficiaries.

This is not related to some form of feminism in its modern sense of a liberating revolt of women, but to a vision which recognises their existence and takes cognisance of it. This enhanced status of women is merely one particular aspect of the gospel at its most essential point, the Good News proclaimed to the poor, whom Jesus sets free as a matter of priority: the disinherited, the outcasts, those reduced to a marginal status, including women and children, pagans and sinners. If Jesus makes such people into privileged members of the fellowship of the children of God, it is not because he is cultivating a sort of masochism. It is not that the prefers what is evil to what is good, or the ugly to the beautiful, but that he discerns, in the poor, values which had been disregarded: be it the precious life of the 'crushed reed' or the unextinguished fire of the 'smouldering wick'.

This basic fact: the invitation extended to women to take a full part in the fellowship of the kingdom, is attested by all four gospels.

2.2. *Limitations in the first two gospels*

However, this fact is blurred in the first two gospels. The group of women disciples of Jesus only appears clearly in two episodes (though these are indeed of fundamental importance): Calvary and the resurrection.

In Mark the women on Easter morning can only 'run away because they were frightened' (Mark 16:8).

Matthew also speaks of their fear, but he qualifies it as an awe which is obviously analogous to that felt by Moses and the prophets at the sudden manifestation of God. He makes it clear, in fact, in a positive sense: 'with awe and great joy they ran to tell the disciples' (Matt. 28:8). This acknowledgment of their witness contradicts Mark 16:8, in which we read that these same women 'said nothing' through fear.

3. THE BREAKTHROUGH OF THE THIRD GOSPEL[6]

3.1. *Women's faith and men's unbelief*

In Luke there is no longer any question of fear. The women are, on the contrary, the prototypes of enthusiasm and courage. Unlike Mark 16:8, the third evangelist contrasts the *belief of the women*, the first witnesses of the empty tomb, with the *unbelief of the apostles* who scorn their 'nonsense' (Luke 24:10-11). It is now the men, instead of the women, who are disparaged.

As for the historical truth of the matter, Luke's interpretation, confirmed by that of Mark and John, squares better with the material fact about which the four evangelists (including Mark) agree: the women came first to the tomb. They were the most faithful, the most courageous. Their fear was not cowardice but a normal religious attitude towards the invisible God: a classic phenomenon in the Bible, as well as in the experience of today.[7]

3.2. *The pioneering role of the women in Luke 1-2*

The initiative taken by the holy women at Calvary and at the resurrection underlines and concludes what Luke tells us of the women, from the (very Lucan) beginning of his gospel. There is the positive attitude of Mary at the annunciation: her fear accompanied by a 'dialectical' pondering, *dialogizeto* (1:29), from which the words *dialogue* and *dialectical* derive. Her question (Luke 1:34) is accepted and honoured; that of Zechariah (1:18) is rejected and punished. The closely parallel diptych of the two announcements in Luke 1 reverses the Pauline principle: 'Women are to remain quiet at meetings'. The priest, blamed for having spoken in the presence of the messenger of God is reduced to silence, struck dumb in the temple in which he officiates (1:20), whereas Mary's question is accepted and receives a reply which is the culminating point of the message (1:35). Mary becomes the Mother of the Messiah Son of God through her free and deliberate consent, in an active commitment as the handmaid of the Lord (Luke 1:38 and 48). She is not *taken* (passively), as in Matt. 1:20, 24; 2:13, 14, 20-21. She actively takes on herself the coming of the Son of God.

Another woman, Elizabeth, precedes her in exercising the gift of prophecy: 'Blessed art thou amongst women' etc. (Luke 1:42-45). Mary prophesies after her, by singing the Magnificat: a song of liberation of extraordinary forcefulness, drawing on Old Testament texts which already expressed this revolution of God, the Magnificat goes beyond them in vigour and coherence. It is significant that the song of the triumph of the poor over the wisdom (1:51), the power (1:52) and the riches (1:53) of this world should be placed in the mouth of a woman, the handmaid of the Lord, who has, as a woman, neither wisdom, power nor possessions.

A little later it is Elizabeth who chooses the name of John the Baptist. His father, Zechariah, dumb and powerless according to the account in Luke 1-2, only confirms it afterwards (Luke 1:62) and only prophesies after some delay: after the women (1:67-79).

Later still, Anna, formally accorded the title of 'prophetess', recognises the Messiah: after Simeon, of course, but prophetism is shown to be both masculine and feminine.

Mary reappears, finally, in the last episode, which is the conclusion of the gospel of Christ's childhood: the rediscovery of Jesus. This final episode already groups all the themes which will be repeated at the end of the gospel as a whole: Jesus lost and found in Jerusalem, his return to the Father, the paschal mystery, etc. Jesus' question to Mary: 'Why were you looking for me?' is similar to that of the two angels to the holy women: 'Why look among the dead for someone who is alive?' And it is indeed the same Jesus who is sought at each of these Passovers. This question is not a reproach: Luke makes it clear that 'Mary stored up these things in her heart' (2:51), not passively, like the man in the parable who buried his talent, but actively. She compares them, according to a *symbolic* process: *comparative examination* of the scripture and the event, which the evangelist renders by the word *symballousa* (Luke 2:19, where he gives expression for the first time to this refrain to the meditation of Mary).

3.3. *The women followers of Jesus*

The most original aspect of the gospel of Luke is that he dares to recognise the holy women as disciples of Christ. This is not a gratuitous extension of the concept on his part. The fact was already attested *in obliquo*, but clearly, by Matthew's reference concerning the burial: these 'women had *followed* Jesus from Galilee, and *served* him' (Matt. 27:55).

Luke gives details of the names of these women whom Matthew describes as not merely *servants* but *followers* of Jesus (this is the theme of the *sequela Christi* which characterises the disciples). He puts them on the same footing as the apostles in 8:1-3: '*The Twelve went with him, as well as certain women*, who had been cured of evil spirits and ailments, Mary, surnamed the Magdalene, from whom seven demons had gone out,

Joanna the wife of Herod's steward Chuza, Susanna, and several others who provided for him out of their own resources.' Admittedly, this text remains ambiguous. Certain authors have stressed the fact that Luke mentions here, in first place, 'women cured of evil spirits', with specific reference to Mary Magdalene, 'from whom seven demons had gone out'. It would thus seem that woman is associated with the powers of darkness. Yet it would be artificial to lay too much stress on this accidental association, for Susanna and Joanna do not seem to belong to the category of sinners and demoniacs.

It is true that the Gospel is the Good News declared to the poor as a matter of priority. And this is one of the reasons for the new attention accorded by Jesus to women. But this call is without respect of persons. Joanna, wife of Chuza, Herod's steward, does not belong to the category of the 'economically deprived'. If the improved status granted to women by Jesus[8] must be included in the general framework of the gospel's enhancement of the status of the poor—all the poor, including sinners—a distinction must be drawn between the latter, whom Jesus has come to cure through conversion, and the poor in spirit, already converted, their lives entirely directed towards the Kingdom, who include, according to Luke 1-2, Mary, Elizabeth, Anna, and doubtless the two holy women mentioned in Luke 8:1-3: those on whom God's favour rests because they live according to true values.

These women who are obviously among the disciples, like the Virgin Mary (Luke 1:38, 45; 2:19 and 51), hear the word of God and keep it (Luke 8:19-21; 11:27-28).

3.4. *Mary, sister of Lazarus: a woman disciple*

Luke makes this point clear in that episode concerning Martha and Mary which he is alone in relating (10:38-42). These women do not belong to the group of wandering disciples who 'follow Jesus' in 8:1-3. What distinguishes them is the *house* in which they entertain Jesus: a point which is common to Luke and John (11:1-40; 12:1-3).

Neither servant nor follower, Mary, sister of Lazarus, is described as occupying the position of the disciple, *'at the feet of Jesus'* (like Paul at the feet of Gamaliel: Acts 22:3). This was a shocking feature: a rabbi, indeed, never accepted a woman as a disciple. And this woman chooses to listen to the Word at the very time when the duties of the household claim her attention. Jesus confirms the choice she has made in liberating herself from the constraints imposed on women at that time. Luke had laid stress on the status of servant of Mary, Mother of Jesus, and of the holy women who 'provided for him out of their own resources' (8:3: who *served* him, as Matthew makes clear in 27:55), but he does not confuse *service* with *servitude*. Mary and the women are servants, as Jesus is a servant (according to Luke in Acts 3:13, 26; 4:27, 30): not in a spirit of alienation but of liberty, which may include liberation from practical service in favour of the 'one thing needed', of the inalienable 'better part' (10:42).

3.5. *Women disciples at Pentecost*

The description of the primitive Church in Acts 1:14 takes up this affirmation and this theme: 'All (the Apostles listed in the previous verse), with one accord, joined in continuous prayer, together with several women including Mary, the Mother of Jesus, and with his brothers.'

Luke intends deliberately to signify that the prototype community of Pentecost is not confined to the Twelve. According to another source he goes on to make it clear in the next verse that it comprises '120 persons' (1:15). Among them he makes very special mention of the women (evidently the women disciples who had followed Jesus in Luke 8:1-3) and Mary his Mother, who is alone mentioned individually. These women will receive the Holy Spirit and the charisma. They will participate in the glossolalia at Pentecost, a point Luke stresses by saying 'They were ALL filled with the Holy Spirit and began to speak foreign languages as the Spirit gave them the gift of speech' (2:4).

4. THE FEMININE ANTHROPOLOGY OF THE FOURTH GOSPEL

4.1. *The dynamic and anticipatory role of the women*

There is more than this in John. Women occupy a significant place, which characterises the very structure of the Fourth Gospel.[9] Each of the three books of John begins with *two* 'feminine' episodes in which women have a role which is not only active and dynamic but anticipatory, with reference to the faith and even to the mysteries of Christ.

Briefly: (1) The *Book of the Signs* begins with Mary's taking the initiative in approaching Christ (2:4) and the servants (2:5), enabling the first sign (*sēmeion*, 2:11) to be performed, which provides the foundation for the faith of the disciples.

Similarly, the Samaritan woman introduces the faith amongst her people (John 4:39-42).

(2) The *Book of the Passion* begins in a similar way with two 'feminine' episodes. The sisters of Lazarus persuade Christ to resurrect their brother, in anticipation of his own resurrection (11:20-32). Mary performs symbolically, in her own house, the prophetic annointing for the sepulchre (12:7).

(3) Finally, the *Book of the Resurrection* begins with the double

episode of Mary Magdalene: she is the first to go to the tomb and makes the other disciples go there (20:1-10). She is the first to see the resurrected Jesus, whom she declares to the disciples (20:11-18).

The role of the women has the same orientation, the same significance, in all six of these episodes, grouped in pairs: an initiative and creativity which forestall, not only the other disciples, but Jesus himself. He seems to be astonished by these anticipations, as he is at the faith of the simple (Luke 8:48), of sinners (Luke 7:50) or of pagans (Luke 7:9; Matt. 15:28) according to the Synoptic Gospels.

4.2. The function of 'the woman' at Calvary

One thing is strange: apart from Mary, Mother of Jesus, none of these women is characterised as a *mother*: there is no hint of an overpowering mother-figure in John. If he describes Mary as *the mother of Jesus* without using her name, *Mary*, he does so without either idealisation, absolutisation or restrictiveness.

In John 19:25-27 Jesus' mother becomes the mother of the ideal disciple by means of a painful transference which is underlined by the subtle grammatical gradation of possessive articles. In 19:25 HIS (Mother) relates her maternity to Jesus; in 19:26 the absence of the possessive, twice replaced by the article THE (Mother) marks a sort of void in the maternal function, before Jesus transfers the possessive to the disciple in 19:27: 'This is YOUR Mother.'

This episode attributes to Mary a function which is very different from the previous ones, being no longer inaugural but central. We are no longer at the beginning, but at the very centre of the *Book of the Passion*; this is the fourth of the seven episodes of Calvary, the central pericope (framed by three pericopes on either side). But this maternal role is not presented from a narrow or individualistic point of view.

Contrary to Semitic usage, Jesus does not call Mary *mother* (John 19:26; see 2:4) but, paradoxically, *woman*, with reference to Gen. 2:22-23 and 3:15 and 20. The relationship of Jesus, the new Adam, to the woman, suggested typologically by John (and perhaps already by Luke 1) has become one of the first central nuclei of the theology concerning the mother of Jesus: notably the profound anthropology of Irenaeus of Lyons in the second century, in which Mary appears as anti-type and repetition (*recirculatio*, or resolution) of Eve.

Mary is presented also as a personification of Israel, *Daughter of Zion*, according to Isaiah 66:7-8, taken up by Rev. 12 and in the Qumran scrolls (1 Qh. III: 9-10). Here Mary illustrates the prophecies of the Old Testament which ascribed value to the eschatological role of woman as mother both of the *Messiah* and of the *new people* of God: the individual person and the collectivity being very closely linked, in line with the cultural structures of Israel.

The maternal function of Mary is not presented here as an exclusive attribute. The new Eve, Daughter of Zion, does not appear as the mother, by contrast with Jesus in the role of the father. Certain Mariologists misread the episode by interpreting it in this hierogamic sense. According to John it is essentially Jesus who gives birth to the Church. She is born of water and the Spirit: from his final breath and from his open side (John 19:30 and 34-35, made more explicit in 1 John 5:6-8). Mary is a feminine and maternal sign, involved in this spiritual event which transcends both masculine and feminine. The maxim that 'there is neither male nor female' which Paul states so firmly, in opposition to the beliefs of his time and his own personal ideas, is attested implicitly in John: a further sign that it comes from Jesus himself, that it is embedded in the inmost structure of his message. One must not, therefore, hypostatise the maternal function of Mary, independently of Christ and of the Spirit he bestows in dying.

5. CONCLUSION

1. The Gospels bear witness to a new attitude of Jesus towards women. He welcomes men and women equally, establishes a personal equality between them, an identity of status which is expressed by the custom of baptising by an identical ritual without distinguishing between the sexes. This revolution appears all the more deliberate in that baptism by immersion presented, in that culture and community, problems of modesty which led Christians to have resource to the services of women for the baptism of women.

2. No explicit formulation of this revolution is found in the words of Christ which have been handed down to us. But this revolution is attested by his attitudes, his praxis, and the very characteristics of the Kingdom which he founded: men and women are received into it on the same footing.

3. This novel aspect of the message of Christ shocked and embarrassed his foes and his disciples themselves. Their preoccupation with apologetics has blurred this aspect of the revolution brought about by the gospel. The last two gospels, freed from this difficulty, reveal the fact better, and give it typologically an anthropological significance, deeply imprinted in the very structure of John's gospel.

4. By considering women with a fresh vision, by calling them to a new place and a new role in the new community, Jesus sets them free, not from without, but from within, by a call to receive, without discrimination, the Word and the gift of the Kingdom. Thus they gained access, on level

terms and without argument, to the baptism of the Holy Spirit, to the baptism of water, and to the Eucharistic Table exactly like men (Acts 1-2; see 10:44; 11:17). Christ's revolution was not achieved by right of conquest, by demands and adversary politics. The gospel does not set out to conquer the powers of this world on their own ground, with their own weapons (constraining power and pressure). It makes its way as an inner surge, a renewal of the heart and of human relationships, which spread from one to another. This method of liberation allows a terminology of humility, even of subordination, to persist in the New Testament. Thus may be explained the parallels between the apparently shocking texts of the New Testament on the obedience of women (1 Cor. 14:34; Eph. 5:22; Col. 3:18; Titus 2:5; 1 Pet. 3:1, compensated for by Eph. 5:21 which inculcates a reciprocal attitude) and the obedience of slaves (Eph. 6:5; Col. 3:22; Titus 2:9; 1 Pet. 2:18, compensated for by Col. 4:1 and Philem.).

5. Beyond the acts and attitudes whereby Christ taught equality and reciprocity between men and women it is important to evaluate theologically the fact that Christ was *born of a woman* and that he lived out the co-relation of man and woman in his relationship with Mary his mother, Mary Magdalene and the others.[10]

The fact of his birth takes on considerable importance at this point. This origin of Christ did not correspond to the expectations of what was, at that time, modern man. The man of *that* time expected, in a more prestigious fashion, a Christ 'who had come down from heaven'; and John feels obliged to satisfy this tendency by applying this expression to Jesus (John 3:13, etc.). That was what appeared noble and carried conviction. Moreover, the only text in which the apostle Paul speaks of the mother of Jesus: 'born of a woman', qualifies this origin in a negative way, as a humiliation which parallels the *dependence* of Jesus with regard to the *Law* (described negatively as a servitude from which one must free oneself in Rom. and Gal.).[11] According to his theology (from which Protestantism drew its inspiration) the Incarnation is *kēnōsis* (Phil. 2:7), an abasement in the flesh, by contrast with the glorious Resurrection. John, on the contrary, followed by Eastern theology, stresses the value of the Incarnation as immediately revelatory and glorious (John 1:13-14; see 1 John 1:1) like the Passion, in which he also discerns the highest point of the glory of Jesus (8:28; 12:32-34; 13:31-32). Although he recognises the opposition between flesh and spirit (6:63) and is haunted by the image of a Christ 'who came down from heaven' (3:13, etc.), he recognises the value of the Incarnation (manifestation of the eternal virgin birth in time: 1:13). At this point, all is already given; and he does not conceive of the relationship of Jesus and his mother as a simply episodic means to an end, but as a living relationship, within the work of

G

salvation. In this sense, he too goes beyond (less clearly than Luke 1:28, 35, 42 and 45) the opposition between the grace of being mother of the Lord according to the flesh and of keeping the Word of God according to the Spirit.[12] In Mary, according to Luke and John, these gifts are linked, as are flesh and spirit in Jesus Christ. It is important that the biblical revelation of the Incarnation involves a relationship between man and woman.

Translated by Lawrence Ginn

Notes

1. Militant feminist writings have hardly made more than a passing reference to Mary, usually to brand this woman as a model of passivity, self-effacement, silence and alienation, an example which is dangerous in three ways. As a virgin, she infers sexual repression and frustration. As a mother (and the supreme example of motherhood) she represents an image of woman reduced to her maternal function, to the detriment of her existence as a person, and of a maternity which is possessive and stifling, which should be done away with at this time of the 'revolt against the mother'. Finally, as virgin-mother, she is a model which is distinctive, contradictory, unrealisable by any other woman and therefore a cause of despair. There is also the additional reproach of idealisation.

However, those feminists who are most knowledgeable about the gospel, particularly Rosemary Radford Ruether, in her latest publications, *Religion and Sexism* (New York 1974) 352 pp.; *New Woman, New Earth: Sexist Ideologies and Human Liberation* (New York 1975) 222 pp., have begun to see very clearly that the picture of Mary in the gospels, especially in Luke 1-2 is quite different; see also Elisabeth Schüssler Fiorenza. On this feminist trend, see R. Laurentin in *La Revue des sciences philosophiques et théologiques* 60 (1976) 459-471and 62 (1978) 278-284.

2. Female circumcision (excision of the clitoris), widely practised in Africa, was not current in biblical lands, but there are grounds for believing that the spirit of the Bible would, in any case, not have permitted it.

3. The history of the Church illustrates this fact. Even at the Council it was the decisions on *ritual* which were discussed at greatest length and which also aroused the greatest reaction, because they were the most pregnant with meaning. The reintroduction of the communion in the chalice for the faithful (which involved, as a natural corollary, a return to the '*Take* and eat' prescribed by Christ—otherwise known as communion in the hand) has had more significance for the restoration of the status of the laity and of the equality of men and women than all the *texts* on the subject. It has given added weight and support to the texts. In the same way, the restoration of concelebration has reversed the tendency towards individualism and restored community life in the liturgy.

4. 'Only Christ sanctifies the dignity of women', according to Léon Xavier-Dufour *Vocabulaire de théologie biblique* (Paris 1970) col. 441. The daily prayer of the Jew proclaims 'Blessed art thou, our God, in that thou hast not made me a gentile, NOR A WOMAN, nor an ignorant man', whereas the woman, for her part, says merely 'Blessed art thou, O Lord, who hast made me according to thy will', as Léon Xavier-Dufour points out. But he recognises that in Israel women, though excluded from worship, are esteemed as equal to men, and sometimes become prophetesses under the influence of the Spirit, e.g., Miriam (Exod. 15:20), Deborah and Jael (Judg. 4:4-5), Huldah (2 Kings 22:14-20), see 1 Cor. 11:5.

One should not, therefore, exaggerate the contrast between Judaism and Christianity on this issue. Apart from the fact that the notion of feminism would be anachronistic in this context, Jesus did not 'come to destroy but to fulfil'. Christian worship did not abolish the wholehearted participation of the primitive community in Jewish temple worship (Acts 2:46; 3:1-3, 8-10; 4:1; 5:20-25, 42) until the accidental break caused by the persecutions: a break which was detrimental to the equilibrium and the vitality of the Christian tradition. The Jewish biblical tradition already implied equality between the sexes, inculcated by the two creation stories: not only the account in P (Gen. 1: 'He created them in the image of himself . . . male and female') but also the vivid account in J (Gen. 2), so strongly reviled by feminists. The aim of the latter text was to witness, against certain ideas which were then current, to the fact that woman shares the same nature as man and is his equal and a helpmate similar to him, in contrast to the animals whose nature is not the same.

5. In the present state of scholarship it has not been established that the baptism of proselytes existed in the time of Christ. It is difficult to say *whether* and *to what extent* this rite (*Tebillah*) related to women. In any case it did not have the character of a rite of initiation, but of purification (for men, after circumcision, before the offering of the sacrifice). It is equally difficult to be precise, in the present state of research, about the participation of women in the various religious initiation rites at the time of Christ: see Goodwater *Women in Antiquity: an annotated bibliography* (Metuchen, N. J. 1975) and L. Swidler *Women in Judaism* (Metuchen (N.) 1976).

The writings of J. Thomas *Le Mouvement baptiste en Palestine et Syrie* (150 B.C. to A.D. 300), Gembloux, Duculot, 1935, and C. Perrot *Le Mouvement baptiste* (Paris, Cours de l'Institut Catholique) 1976 (on the period between the Old and New Testaments), do not pay much attention to the problem of female participation. Perrot stresses only (p. 25) that the 'baptism of proselytes is not a rite of admission' (unlike circumcision) and that ' "in good Jewish theology" one does not base arguments on the particular example of women'.

6. Luke is in every way later than Mark whom he uses, and probably later than Matthew. A long exegetical tradition agreed that he wrote around the year A.D. 80. New theories date the Gospels much earlier: from A.D. 50-60 for the Synoptics (e.g., Carmignac and the Anglican Bishop J. A. T. Robinson [author of *Honest to God*]).

7. The ending of Mark (canonical, but not written by Mark himself) bears witness to the fact that Mary of Magdala was blessed with the first appearance of

the resurrected Jesus (16:9). Thus three canonical gospels testify that the women were the first beneficiaries of the appearance of Christ, and the first to witness to it. Paradoxically, Luke, who is elsewhere most sensitive to the role of the women, is the only one who attributes no appearance of the risen Christ to them, but only that of two angels (Luke 24:4 and 23, where the word *angel* appears).

8. This rise in the status of women is found notably in the text where Jesus protests against discrimination regarding divorce according to the law (Mark 10:11): his emphasis on the defence of women is shown by the complement *ep'auten*, which should be translated *against* her.

9. André Laurentin *Doxa* (Paris) vol. 3 (unpublished) has studied this fascinating structure.

10. The opinion of W. E. Phipps, according to which Jesus was married (*Was Jesus married?* [New York 1970]), a theory spread abroad by various writers and novelists eager to shock their readers, has no serious historical value and runs counter to the words of Jesus on celibacy for the sake of the Kingdom (R. Laurentin, in *La Revue des sciences philosophiques et théologiques* 60 (1976) 479.

11. In Gal. 4:4 Paul employs not the verb to be born, *Gennao*, but to become (*gignomai*): a nuance which is not without importance.

12. R. E. Brown *The Birth of the Messiah* has understood very perceptively that at this point there was a contradiction to be overcome. He has clearly identified the key concepts and texts, but the origin which he proposes is factitious (see R. Laurentin, in *La Revue des sciences philosophiques et théologiques* 60 (1976) 311-314, and 62 (1978) 99-101).

PART IV

New Beginnings

Manuel Alcalá

The Challenge of
Women's Liberation to
Theology and Church Reform

1. THE SITUATION

THEOLOGY and the life of the Church continually feel the impact of the evolution of human history. This is normal and right. If it did not happen, theology would degenerate into science fiction and the life of the Church would go into hibernation, which is contrary to the Spirit of Christ.

This impact may vary greatly both in intensity and quality. Sometimes it causes serious difficulties and even head-on conflicts. This happened in the case of the confrontation of the first Judaeo-Christian communities with the pagan world around them. At other times it may be a short term stimulus or check on the Church. But then there are occasions in which this impact is a real challenge to tradition, which is too slow to assimilate the development, resulting in a severe crisis and many confrontations of all kinds.

Among the many historical movements which have recently had the greatest impact on theology and the life of the Church, women's liberation is one of the most important. By this we mean a growing awareness whose primary aim to do away with the centuries of sexual discrimination both in society and the Church. It demands the recognition of women in society as equal to men as full human persons, and in the Church as daughters of God, responsible and creative adults.

Women's liberation, whose complicated history we are unable to go into now, began by being a pre-scientific fact. It had the character of a sociological 'ethos', that is to say, a style and way of life different from the traditional, which by either violent or non-violent means, by consent or through confrontation, progressively invaded various circles of public life, especially the political, social and cultural.

Religious circles, especially the Catholics, were from the first reserved and distrustful of the women's liberation movements. The reactions both of the papal magisterium and theology, were generally negative, not only when the movement first arose and grew in the second half of the nineteenth century, but late on into the twentieth. There were many reasons for this antagonism. The three most important were of course the facts that the movement had arisen in society outside the Church and its aims were secular; the movement grew fastest in countries which were mainly Protestant rather than Catholic; and thirdly that the movement was progressive and even revolutionary at least in some of its ramifications.

Pope Pius XII (1939-1958) was certainly aware of the phenomenon, especially after the second world war and alluded to it in various speeches. However he appeared to support it only in civil (rather than ecclesiastical) life. The first explicit statements of the Church came with the beginning of Vatican II, but during the reign of John XXIII (1958-1963) they were timid and hesitant. The open confrontation and challenge to the Church came in the post-conciliar period during the pontificate of Paul VI (1963-1978). The conflict appeared in many forms and places, from more or less important happenings in various local churches undergoing the influence of secularisation, to interventions by the hierarchy, especially in the 1969, 1971 and 1974 sessions of the Roman episcopal Synod.

Catholic theology went through a similar process. At first the subject was conspicuous by its absence or cursorily dismissed. Its bibliography was meagre and nearly always the work of Protestant authors. One significant example is enough to illustrate this: J. P. Migne (1800-1875) in his condemnation of 'mulierosos, sive veteres sive recentiores haereticos',[1] with reference to the ordination of women. Later the Code of Canon Law (1919) with its many canons discriminating against women, seemed to dismiss the problem finally. There was the same failure to take seriously, not only theological opinions on the ordination of women, but also the deficient historical interpretation of the female diaconate in the early Church.

Today however, there is a large bibliography on the subject of women in the Church.[2] Questions have re-arisen with renewed urgency, showing that the problem is still very much alive and has not been resolved, although at first sight the contrary may appear to be the case. Even the recent Declaration Inter Insigniores (1977) of the Sacred Congregation for the Doctrine of the Faith does not give a definitive answer. It is a simple statement of the law, without detail or interpretation, with crucial omissions and only a partial presentation of tradition. This only served to sharpen the debate.[3] This is why we are devoting this article to this important subject, in spite of the fact that limited space will inevitably prevent full treatment of it.

2. STIMULUS AND CHALLENGE TO THEOLOGY

In future Catholic theology, while maintaining adequate links with the magisterium of the Church, ought to use its own particular methods to reformulate the question of women's liberation and feminism in relation to the doctrine of God. Of course this requires the revision of a great deal of the Judaeo-Christian tradition, which has always been anti-feminist because of its androcentric, masculinist and even machistic view of the world. The chief aim must be a double one: firstly, carefully to distinguish what constitutes genuine divine revelation, strictly speaking, among the assembly of socio-cultural and religious traditions in which this revelation was in fact made. Secondly, to study the scope of the Church's power and the legitimacy of such a power to create new traditions which for various reasons have not existed up till now.

This double process is extremely difficult, not just because of the labour of returning to the sources with a new point of view, but because it requires a change of attitude.

In the field of *general history* there needs to be progress in the study of religious contemporary with the Mosaic, to discern the negative influence of their sexual politics, fertility cuts, sacred prostitution etc., which resulted in the idea of woman as a sub-person related to the powers of darkness. There should also be an investigation of patriarchal attitudes in the pastoral world, the androcentric view of sexuality which predominates in the liturgy and socio-religious leadership.

In the field of *Holy Scripture* exegesis should continue its work on literary forms, dismissing once and for all in the *Old Testament* the literalist reading of the first chapters of Genesis, which have been of crucial importance in the discrimination against women in Jewish tradition. In particular the fact that in the story the man is the protagonist in creation and the women in original sin. The true meaning of human bi-sexuality should be clarified, with its double reflection of God and the way it offers for pre-sacramental dialogue with God. Greater importance should be given to the female prophetic figures of the Old Covenant, the concept of Wisdom and the relationship between God and his people symbolised by marriage. In the *New Testament* textual criticism of the Pauline and Deutero-Pauline texts is required. They must be cleared of montanist interpolations, which had such a great influence on later feminist trends both patristic and canonist and scholastic. Then Paul's ambiguous position towards women and their ministerial collaboration in the preaching of the gospel could be clarified. Of decisive importance is the study of the behaviour of Jesus towards women, the 'signs' of the Kingdom in relation to them and their part in the first news of the resurrection.

In the field of *dogma* the image of God must be re-examined from a feminine dimension. This will affect the doctrine of the Trinity and especially that of the Spirit. Attempts to do this up till now have been vary cautious.[4]

We have already referred to the opposition between grace and sin in the Old Testament. Feminist revision is badly needed in *soteriology*. One of the most important aspects would be the study of sin in relation to *Christology* and *Mariology*. In Christology the meaning of Christ's masculinity needs clarifying as well as his position as head of the mystical body and his mystical nuptial relationship with the Church. There is still a great deal of work to be done on the figure of Mary, even though she has been much discussed in recent decades. We are surprised by the conservative attitude of some specialists who prefer to stress the symbolic side and, as far as we know, have not paid the same attention to Mary's feminity, her sharing as co-redemptrix as woman and mother of God, and her unique position in the history of salvation. Stress needs to be laid on her womanhood and active companionship with her male Son in the work of universal redemption.[5]

In the field of *ecclesiology* more work needs to be done on Jesus' awareness both of his divine sonship and of the foundation of the Church. There must be a move from the ecstatic to a more dynamic vision. This has direct repercussion on the field of *sacramentology*. Here clarification is essential on the position of women with regard to the sacraments, services and ministries. The sacramental status of the diaconate needs to be clarified. In particular it must be determined whether the *cheirotoneia*, the laying on of hands, given to Christian deaconesses for several centuries was a true sacrament in our later terminology, or just a blessing, and whether women formed part of the clergy in the specific sense.[6] These are essential points for the description of the feminine ministry, beginning with the order of widows and their possible access to the priesthood in more than the purely generic sense. Of course this investigation refers back to the image of the priesthood of Christ and the New Testament. We also have to clear the mist which envelops the development of the triad: deacon, presbyter, bishop and the great ones in the Church in the structuring of the sacrament of order. To be brief, the exact meaning of episcopal leadership in the Christian community must also be clarified, with its linking to the masculine in its acts '*in persona Christi*' and '*in persona Ecclesiae*'.

In the field of *theological anthropology* further investigation is needed into human sexuality as a symbol and as 'sacramental', in order to destroy ancient and modern taboos about this 'existential' radical part of human nature and its openness to the supernatural.

In the field of *canon law* discrimination against women should be traced back to its beginnings and the role of Roman Law in this discrimination determined, as well as that of mediaeval compilers, the decretists and decretalists who were chiefly responsible for the formation of the *Corpus Juris Canonici* and its later elaboration in the Codex. This could have a strong effect on the current revision of the latter.[7]

Finally in the field of *history of Christian ideas* and *Church history* it is very important that there should be a reappraisal of feminine ministries, beginning with the order of widows and deaconesses, as active and proto-typical institutions for preaching the gospel. Then the conflict between the ecclesiastical hierarchy and feminist movements, both heretical and schismatic, must be examined to discover what is specifically against the Church's teaching in them.

Within such a study greater attention would be paid to the origins of consecrated virginity and also to the influence of clerical celibacy on feminist ideas and abuses of the 'third way'.

The field of *ecumenical theology* is of great importance at the moment and here an analysis is required of feminism in the different Christian confessions: Orthodox, Protestant, and especially, Anglican.[8] The fact that the latter has radically modified its position with regard to women in the priesthood is a real challenge, not only because of its biblical motivations, but because of the difficulty it could give rise to in the attempt to regain unity.

As can be seen from this necessarily incomplete survey, feminism requires not only serious theological thought but also presents a real threat to many past attitudes. An adequate treatment of it requires a genuine *metanoia* or theological change of mind. The first step is to recognise that the subject is of great importance for the future of the science of God and its repercussions in the life of the Church.

3. STIMULUS AND CHALLENGE TO CHURCH REFORM

In Vatican II the Catholic Church proclaimed to the world the need for constant self-correction and self-renewal. This is especially important when the Church is facing radically new problems. Feminism is one of these, as we shall now show.

In the first place there has been a *fundamental change in the situation*. Women have gradually penetrated ecclesiastical areas and structures from which they were prohibited in the past. In *teaching* the presence of women is common today from the simplest catechism class to the highest theological levels. Promotion in the secular world has made it possible for women, with complete orthodoxy and the explicit although more or less cautious approbation of the hierarchy, to hold professorships and even posts as deans in faculties of theology. The same is true of the *ministry*. For many reasons, and in particular the shortage of priests, there are numerous women, both nuns and others, throughout the Church who fulfil the functions of non-ordained ministries. There are readers, acolytes, distributors of the Eucharist, preachers, including preachers of the Sunday sermon, women who baptise and preside at funerals, etc. *At a tangent from ecclesial direction* there are women who are almost parish priests, almost archpriests, visitors delegated by the bishop, present at diocesan councils, etc.

A second important point is the *paradoxical difference* between this situation and current legislation. Leaving aside the *Codex Juris Canonici* and its obsolete canons, and looking only at the post-conciliar period, it is extraordinary that Paul VI's 'motu proprio' *Ministeria Quaedam* (1972) which deals with the reform of minor orders, the change of name to 'ministries' and their reduction to 'reader' and 'acolyte' (with the important innovation that they can be conferred on laymen who are not candidates for ordination to the priesthood), reserves these posts for men 'according to the venerable tradition of the Church'. The reason for this is not clear, because the tradition referred to the clergy. It introduces a discrimination into lay life which is damaging to these ministries. It is also completely out of date because the specific functions of these ministries, and higher ones too, have been fulfilled by women for many years. Similar paradoxes throughout the world have given rise to explanatory notes from various episcopal conferences and, unofficially, from the Vatican itself. The problem was deferred and not solved. This difference between the actual situation and the law is growing greater rather than smaller and there is the danger of a serious split, hypocrisy and loss of ecclesiastical authority.

There must be radical revision, that is to say, reform. This is not an easy task, even for those who freely admit that the Church itself through the decisions of its authentic *magisterium* has the authority to decide what is changeable and what is not in its own structure. Because the question has not been solved and because it is so radically new, even the genuine *magisterium* is probably not aware of the scope of its jurisdiction. Recourse to the safest opinion, as happened in the Declaration *Inter Insigniores* does not make this opinion either definitive or even true doctrine. If Christian women in the early centuries had performed functions in the Church they do today, they would certainly have been considered heretical. Their behaviour would have been called a breaking away from Christian belief. In fact it would not have been, even though many people today think that it is. Historical change throws light on the past and this sometimes gives a clearer insight into the Church's nature. But for this new clarity, the authentic *magisterium* needs the help of theology.

From the practical point of view we think the following points are important, both for the effect they might have on theology and on change in the life of the Church, while we are awaiting a definitive decision from the authentic *magisterium*.

1. Encouragement of theology done by women and from their point of view, so that more can be said about areas which are inaccessible to abstract reflection and choked with anti-feminism.

2. The promotion by legitimate authority of new feminine ministries to the farthest possible extent and urgent restoration of the female diaconate with laying on of hands or *cheirotoneia*. This, which is in accordance with the practice of the early Church would not only clarify the sacramental meaning of this ministry but also be the basis for reviewing the question of possible ordination of women to the priesthood.

3. Putting this forward as a subject for treatment by the episcopal Synod. This would require previous study by the relevant Congregation, Commissions and Pontifical Secretariats.

These measures taken at the level of the universal Church together with local initiatives, would make people aware that feminism is an event in which the Christian community can show its fidelity to Christ, to itself and to the world.

Translated by Dinah Livingstone

Notes

1. J. P. Migne *Cursus completus theologiae* (Paris 1840) XXV p. 53.

2. M. Alcalá *La mujer y los ministerios en la Iglesia* (Madrid 1979). This contains a bibliography from Vatican II until 1978.

3. L. and A. Swidler (eds.) *Women Priests. A Catholic Commentary on the Vatican Declaration* (New York 1977).

4. See for example, A. Greely *The Mary Myth* (New York 1977).

5. See the large bibliography in Sociedad Mariologica Española *Enciclopedia mariana posconciliar* (Madrid 1975).

6. C. Vagaggini 'L'ordiniazione delle diaconesse nella tradizione graeca e bizantina' *Orientalia christiana periodica* 40 (1974) 145-189.

7. I. Raming *Der Ausschluss der Frau vom priesterlichem Amt. Gottgewollte Tradition oder Diskriminierung?* (Cologne 1973); J. Bosch 'El ministerio de la mujer en las Iglesias cristianas. Para la formacion de un dossier ecumenico' *Escritos del Vedat* 4 (1974) 199-203.

Margaret Brennan

Women and Men
in Church Office

THE VIETNAMESE poet Thich Nhat Hahn wrote somewhere that 'it is the path of return which continues the journey'. For me, these words provide a kind of key to any consideration about new directions or initiatives that will bring women as partners with men in Church office.

It is not the kind of return that attempts to reproduce a place and time within a culture and circumstances long past, but one which asks us to return with our experience of the centuries to the sources of life from which the Church began its journey and to understand them anew in their perennial possibility.

In developing the topic of women and men in Church office then, I will return first to the New Testament foundations and from them pose some possibilities that confront the crisis of the present and the challenge of the future.

1. NEW TESTAMENT FOUNDATIONS

An indispensable element in any consideration of women and men in Church office is to begin with the mission and ministry of Jesus as the ultimate norm of any new shaping of ministry. Scriptural exegesis today suggests that Jesus' understanding of his mission took on a deepened awareness through a profound religious experience in his baptism at the Jordan. An understanding of his identity in relation to God as to his ultimate source broke in on him with a force and an intimacy that has changed and charged the destination of all humankind.

Led by the Spirit of God to the desert, Jesus met the deceiver, and a new creation story was enacted. The temptation to deny death, to be like God, to control life were faced again by humanity in Jesus. But unlike the first man and woman, Jesus resisted preserving himself at all costs, and in his struggle unto death we have learned forever that God is faithful. We have learned as well that the need to dominate and oppress one another for power and control is the deception that continues to challenge the plan and providence of God who calls us to the formation of the divine-human community. This community is to be marked by mutuality and partnership whereby we respect the dignity of one another, and through the complementarity of gifts the work of creation continues on this earth that we are given to tend and to develop.

The mission of Jesus in the gospel of Luke begins with a stark proclamation. Jesus, seated in the synagogue, reads a prophetic text of consolation, declaring that this word has come true today—and that it has come true in him (Luke 4:16-22). Jesus carried out this expression of his mission concretely through ministry. Teaching, healing, closing the gaps, lifting the burdens of oppression—reconciliation is the meaning of that ministry. In his life that is reconciliation, Jesus is telling us who God is—the tender, loving, compassionate father and mother of human persons called to the same life, holiness, and personal dignity. The mission and ministry of Jesus is the ultimate norm of all Church ministry.

In the cultural situation of Jesus' times, women were among those marginated by the male domination of the patriarchal society. Rabbinical tradition in general manifested a profound contempt for women and stipulated more than once that their witness could not be received.[1] Moreover, adult male Jews thanked God in prayer for not having made them gentiles, women, or slaves.[2]

Jesus' attitudes toward women, his reverence and acceptance of them has been pointed out elsewhere in this issue and so needs no articulation here. But what does command our attention is that the tradition of Jesus regarding women echoes the word of Genesis that women and men alike are created in the image and likeness of God, entrusted equally with the same dignity and gifted with the same abilities in the on-going creation of the world. A reading of the four gospels shows clearly that women were among the followers of Jesus, shared in his ministry, stood by him in his death, witnessed to his resurrection, and were entrusted with the proclamation of his risen life. Scripture scholars point out that women met the qualifications of apostles laid down by both Luke and Paul.[3]

The letters of Paul give striking testimony to the ministry of women. Phoebe 'a helper of many and of myself as well',[4] was a woman who opened her house for religious meetings. These households were the centres of the Christian community in Corinth, places of worship and hospitality. The women of such households were influential and apparently ministered in mutuality and partnership with their husbands. In Corinth, likewise, Paul met Prisca and Aquila, a Jewish couple, religious political refugees from Italy. They were a couple whom Paul calls his 'fellow-workers' in Christ Jesus—associating himself with them in the ministry of evangelisation. They not only travelled with him to Ephesus but risked death to save his life, and as Phoebe, opened their home as a meeting place for the Christian community.[5]

In other letters Paul singles out and greets other women who 'worked hard' co-operating in his aspostolic mission.[6] In Philippians, he calls to mind Evodia and Syntyche who 'have laboured side by side with me in the gospel together with Clement and the rest of my fellow-workers'.[7]

The references to the ministry of women, to the mutuality and partnership through which they were closely associated with Paul and his fellow-workers, give testimony to the internalisation of the tradition of Jesus expressed in Gal. 3:28, that in Christ Jesus there is no distinction of status, of race, of sex. All baptised Christians have received the Spirit and are empowered by that same Spirit to proclaim the 'magnalia Dei', the great works of God. If indeed it is true that Gal. 3:28 is a baptismal formulation cited by Paul, then by reciting it, as Elizabeth Fiorenza points out, 'the newly initiated Christians expressed their self-understanding over and against the societal-religious creeds of their surrounding Graeco-Roman culture' and 'affirmed at their baptism that all religious-patriarchal distinctions were abolished in Jesus Christ'.[8] 'This new self-understanding,' Fiorenza asserts, 'allowed not only gentiles and slaves to assume leadership in the Christian movement but also women.'[9]

Such New Testament references show that women were not marginal in the community, but rather exercised leadership as co-workers in the ministry of evangelisation.

In the light of such striking testimony in the early Church about mutuality and partnership in ministry, it is surprising that within a few decades this mutuality totally disappeared by the emergence of the male clerical model that so dominated and eventually controlled all the ministries of the Church. In fact such testimony is completely overshadowed in interpretation by the later interpolations added to the First Letter of Paul to the Corinthians that 'women should keep silence in the churches' (14:34) and the plagiarisation of this text in the First Pastoral Letter to Timothy (2:11-14) which forbids women to teach because they were created after men and they are responsible for original sin.

What reasons can be suggested for such a change apparent in the New Testament itself? Current scholarly research in the cultural patterns of the early decades of Christianity indicate that the almost immediate insertion of the Christian community within the Graeco-Roman culture posed serious problems and pressures of adaptation and acculturalisation. Roger Gryson in his study on *The Ministry of Women in the Early Church*, while acknowledging the important role of women in the primitive Christian community, suggests that the lack of leadership and liturgical office or public role afforded to them came not so much from the example of Jesus who did not choose them as apostles, but rather from the situation of women in the Graeco-Roman world—a situation which allowed them little place of any kind in public ministry. He suggests further, that to have called women forth to a role which was foreign to the culture in which the Church had inserted itself would have demanded a far more prophetic charism than the times demanded. Moreover, he notes that we would need to be in touch with the understanding that women had of themselves, an area in which we still have insufficient data for reflection.[10]

To take seriously the full implications and meaning of Gal. 3:28 in such a socio-cultural climate would have been a revolutionary stance for the Christian communities that developed within the framework of the Roman world. The functioning of the Empire was established in part on the stability of household codes that provided order and a hierarchy of relationships between slave and free, men and women, citizen and alien. The early Christian movement, on the other hand, testifies to the belief in and creation of a society in which all distinctions between race and sex are dissolved.

The supposition that the early Christians adopted the framework of the Graeco-Roman world in their own acculturalisation is reflected in several Pauline letters where the contradiction between the basic tenet of the tradition of Jesus regarding the equality of all persons and its compromise within the highly patriarchal society of the Graeco-Roman world, is clearly indicated as was pointed out earlier. In time, such cultural expression reflected in the Pauline letters—especially as applied to women, took on the character of revealed teaching and influenced the continued structures and institutional development of the Church.

It is evident then from New Testament literature, that the resurrection faith, as shared in the early Christian communities became more or less structured. The earliest Christian communities were less structured and governed more directly by the authority of the apostles (eye-witnesses of the resurrection), by the experience of the Spirit and the charismata (the gifts in the community). Women, as has been seen, were part of this experience. Later, the Christian communities were structured more by authority moving directly towards what we call Church order due to cultural differentiation, heresy, etc. Still later, but still in New Testament times, this authority assumed the hierarchical structure of *episkopos*/presbyter. The result, with the passage of time, was the controlling of ministries by the hierarchy and the development of an unfortunate gap or separation between clergy and laity.

Church order, that is, the organisation of ministries in the community, is surely important and even indispensable. But, it is crucial to realise that Church order, while rooted in the tradition of Jesus, is post-Jesus, historically constituted, and is in no way absolute, that is, exclusively of divine origin. Church order was the creation of the believing community to respond practically to its actual needs in its effort to live out the mission and ministry of Jesus, as handed on.

We can conclude therefore, that there must always be flexibility in the organisation of Church ministries in order to meet continuing, new and practical demands of the Christian communities' efforts to live the mission and ministry of Jesus as handed on. And, we can hope as well, that in adjusting to new cultural situations the Church will not be compromised by existing structures or ideologies. The long history of the Church gives testimony to the continual struggle with the dilemma of refusing to preserve its life and its most fundamental belief, and the compromising of it on the other hand, so as to keep its life and proclaim its message in this world.

Whether or not the early Christian Church could have stood over against such a highly-established structure of the Graeco-Roman world with regard to women is debatable. Nevertheless, the compromising of its basic tenet of full equality among all persons who are one in the same Spirit of the risen Lord, does contradict, or at least make ambiguous the stance of Jesus who did not preserve his own life in the commitment to his own mission of forming the divine-human community.

2. THE PRESENT AS A SITUATION OF CRISIS AND CHALLENGE

Such cultural compromises have surely affected the Church both in its understanding of ministry and the witness of that diversity of gifts which call all baptised persons to that mutuality and partnering which enhance and give witness and variety to its mission.

It is the contention of Bernard Cooke that the development of the clergy-laity division over the centuries, together with the control of ministries by the hierarchy, has impoverished the Church and left the laity in a position of passivity and powerlessness. Their ministerial gifts for the most part remained dormant and undeveloped.[11] For women, this situation has been particularly debilitating. Not only are they among the laity, but as women, they are unable, even if gifted and called to partner with any mutuality in ministering to the mission, barred, because they are women, from any public, official function in the proclamation of the Good News which has been the sole prerogative of male, celibate clerics.

The Church of the Vatican Council II drew us back sharply to the tradition of Jesus in articulating the nature of its life and mission today. Vatican II has invited us once again to consider the Galatian text on equality and has called all Christians once again to the realisation that they enjoy the same vocation to holiness and to a mutual responsibility for the saving mission of the Church.

Such basic teachings, however, are placed within other statements that continue the tendency to confuse as well as compromise the actualisation of such a truth by preserving the structures that make its realisation difficult if not impossible. Many of these compromises are reflective of socio-cultural phenomena that continue to institutionalise inequality and consequent systemic oppression in patriarchal attitudes that subtly, often unconsciously, and sometimes sacrosanctly enshrine them.

Might it not be that an ecclesiology of the future needs to be open to a total reconsideration of Church order because of entirely new needs, entirely new cultural experiences and awarenesses and the actual knowledge we have today of cultural differentiation? This new knowledge is of such a nature that it does not permit us any longer to ignore or avoid or be complacent with present Church order as the one which best serves the mission and ministry of Jesus. Women, and more to the point still, the laity, must be a part of this re-ordering of Church structures.

It is evident that there are many ramifications of such a radical change in Church ordering according to cultural differentiation.

One such ramification might concern what we mean by ordination. It might well be that ordination itself, as an element of Church order, must be re-thought, loosened perhaps from its present status as corner-stone, spinal cord, or central element of Church order, and made more flexible in form to meet new needs, new situations, the facticity of cultural differentiation, of global awareness.

The New Testament itself shows great diversity in this regard, that is, over those ministries that had authority in the community. Today, for example, we might ask whether or not there should be any permanent ordination based on an ontological theology of orders.

Perhaps there should be new forms of commissioning according to new tasks, to be exercised for a specific time, in a specific community and only after the gifts have been tested in the community, for example, lay-leaders in communities might be designated as the president of the Eucharist for a particular time and need.

Within such a refashioning, a revisioning, women have a central place, following from gifts such as building up the community etc. Ministry should increasingly become a partnering, a complementary of gifts in expressing and actualising the mission and ministry of Jesus. Therefore, ordination, commissioning to ministry, as an important and indispensable part of Church order, must also be rethought in terms of new needs, new cultural differentiation. It must also include those whom the community recognises and calls as gifted to lead the community in the ritualisation of those human graced moments in life in which the human experience of Jesus touches our own in a profound way. Such expression, it would seem, should actualise the complementarity of the whole human family—male and female, lay and religious.

In summary it would seem that the ecclesiology we need in the future, in order to have a renewed priestly ministry and to include the recognition of orders for women's ministerial call, must renew its belief and understanding that the shared faith experience of the Christian community is a source of on-going revelation. It must become even more explicit than it is now, due to entirely new pastoral needs: ethnic, racial, Third and Fourth Worlds etc. The realisation of such an ecclesiology calls for a new Church order in the best sense of the tradition. It is one that calls for a stronger local church autonomy in which the role of the laity (including women) be given greater responsibility and full recognition proportionate to cultural awareness. As Westerners, it calls for a realisation as to how our understanding of Church order has diminished the Church, distorted our understanding of mission and challenges us to find a whole new set of symbols which express our reality.

New models of community and life styles within the Church and new models of partnering in ministry that overcome the old dichotomies of male-female, clergy-laity are the challenging consequence of such considerations.

'Partnership,' writes Letty Russell, 'does have a future, just as it has a present and a past. It has a future because God has chosen to be partners with us, chosen to be present in our lives through Jesus Christ as a happening of co-humanity.'[12]

If we believe the Church is the divine-human community enspirited with Jesus' risen life, then, as Jesus, it must not court the temptation to compromise its saving mission by the continuation of structures that dominate and control the full exercise of the gifts of women and men as well as clerics.

The critical juncture at which the world stands makes such mutuality an imperative if we are to do theology, to move forward the mission of the Church in a way that can be creative of a more truly human community of love, justice, and liberation. For as St Paul writes: 'When anyone is united to Christ, there is a new world; the old order is gone, and a new order has already begun' (2 Cor. 5:17).

Notes

1. See Roger Gryson *The Ministry of Women in the Early Church* (Minnesota 1976) p. 113.

2. Elisabeth S. Fiorenza 'Women in the Early Christian Movement' *Women Spirit Rising* ed. Carol P. Christ and Judith Ploskow (San Francisco 1979) p. 89.

3. *Ibid.* p. 89.

4. Rom. 16:1-2.

5. Rom. 16:5; I Cor. 16:19.

6. Rom. 16:12.

7. Phil. 4:2-3.

8. In the article cited in note 2.

9. In the same article cited in note 2.

10. See *The Ministry of Women* cited in note 1 at pp. 109-120.

11. See Bernard Cooke *Ministry to Word and Sacraments* (Philadelphia 1976) pp. 63-64, 205-206, 265-266.

12. Letty M. Russell *The Future of Partnership* (Philadelphia 1979) p. 159.

Catherina Halkes

Feminist Theology:
An Interim Assessment[1]

1. HOW CAN WE DEFINE FEMINIST THEOLOGY?

BY AND LARGE, feminist theology is a reaction and a protest provoked by a theology which for many centuries took for granted that
reality had its centre in the male of the species. It was based on scriptures
which were written in terms of a patriarchal mentality and flourished in a
male-dominated culture and a hierarchically structured Church. In this
perspective the two outstanding representatives of classical theology,
Augustine and Thomas Aquinas, dominated the theological scene so far
as Catholic theology is concerned.

Here Christian anthropology is no doubt primarily concerned with the
relation between man and God. But inevitably it also has to deal with the
mutual relationship between man and woman. And while, on the level of
grace, woman and man are equal, in creation woman is subordinated to
man.[2]

It is true that during the last fifty years new theologies have sprung up
which brought out the changed relationship between man (and woman)
and God. Yet, however 'revolutionary' these new trends were, as in
political theology or the theology of liberation, women still play no part in
them. They simply do not appear or it is taken for granted that they are
subordinate.

1.1. Feminist theology could therefore possibly be described as a
theology which concentrates on the relationship between man and
woman and on finding a proper theological expression of this. This issue
can only become really relevant by re-examining our historically and
culturally conditioned image of humanity, of mankind. How exactly are

the two sexes related to humanity as such, to what is essentially human? Such a theology could obviously be opposed to any theology which starts from assuming that the functions of man and woman have been fixed once and for all by creation and to any culture which is congenitally determined to preserve these two patterns. Even a theologian like Karl Barth failed to escape from this narrow view of humanity.[3] To examine all this, to bring it out into the open and to correct it is a way of defining feminist theology as a possible first approach.

1.2. Another approach is that which sees the origin of feminist theology in the dissatisfaction of women who have found out that existing doctrine continues the injustice of demeaning women by reducing their status and keeping them in their place. Women, those 'banished children of Eve', are banned from the altar, i.e., from the sacred, as well as from the history and the intellectual world of mankind. Now that they are beginning to discover their own rights and values, they are straightening their backs and arriving at a *recta confessio*, a re-shaping of traditional doctrine and theology.[4]

1.3. In a broader sense feminist theology can be described as a contextual theology. Here the historical aspect plays an important part: the too generalised and over-emphasised characteristics of man and woman are being eroded and people begin to sense the vast potential contained in the various aptitudes and images of woman as such. Contextual theology is as much involved in the present state of the world as in history. It has nothing relevant to say if it is not alive to the socio-cultural, political and economic factors which demand a very careful analysis. I also want to refer here to the theology of the 'signs of the times' in the documents of Vatican II.

With this in mind, feminist theology has seriously to consider the significance of the fast-growing women's liberation movement and its 'revelationary' character. And this it has to tackle 'diachronically', i.e., throughout history (how much were salvation and Church history a matter of 'him' rather than of 'her'?) as well as 'synchronically', which means bringing out the present in all its complexity.

All this means that we have to drop the universal idea of 'woman' because it is too abstract and ignores history. It also means that we should avoid generalising about 'women' as if they were a clear-cut caste, homogeneous and easy to generalise about. The context of women's relations with each other and their corresponding experiences reveal too many variations.

Even within the very limited context of the Netherlands, I simply cannot as a white, middle-class and intellectual woman, living in a capitalist society, speak for my sisters who belong to a proletariat which remains with us, nor for the world of the labouring class, nor for the prostitutes, the women from Surinam, nor for the wives of immigrant labourers. Nor do I dare to identify myself with the coloured women from the Third World who fight the battle for their class and/or race together with their male partners and perhaps find it even difficult to see us as their sisters because we live in an affluent society and in structures which maintain their oppression.

1.4. Another description of feminist theology comes in my view closer to the heart of the matter, and this is what is called the 'genitive theology'. This theology, one has to admit, is manipulated and interpreted in various ways.[5] In so far as I am concerned, I see it this way: if the 'genitive' is seen as *subjective*, one might say that now, for the first time and in the concrete, woman is seen as the *subject of* living her own experience of the faith, of the formulation of that faith and the reflection upon this, and therefore theologising about it. But this obviously only holds for those women who have shaken off their subservience, have rid themselves of the subconscious urge to imitate the male (for fear of being 'left out') and have repudiated the image the male has projected on them. These women are no longer interested in finding out 'Who am I expected to be?' but rather in 'Who am I?' This last point is common to all feminists, however varied their situation: they all want to establish their identity as persons in their own right.

All this means that there is a whole group of women who do not *want* to play the personal and active part implied in the term 'subjective genitive theology'. They are the women who have deliberately opted for that uncritical pattern of women's liberation which has 'liberated' them in the sense that they feel free to infiltrate effectively into a society where the existing norms, values and even scientific endeavour are dominated by the male.

There is another group of women for whom this kind of theology is meaningless because they are *incapable* of understanding it. These are the women who have so completely absorbed and adapted themselves to the still current images of 'woman', the stereotype pattern, functions and expectations of 'woman', that they do not even realise how unfree they are.

If 'genitive theology' is taken as implying the *objective* genitive then the object of feminist theology is the way in which the protesting women live their faith, deal with scripture and tradition, how they experience God: Creator, Redeemer, Spirit; how they understand their humanity and their sexuality, and the restrictions imposed upon them by structures which render them powerless. These two aspects of genitive theology (subjective and objective) are so closely intertwined that it is almost imposs-ible to separate them, the reason obviously being that these kinds of experiences of women will be more adequately understood and expressed by women, and it is women who are both the subject and the object of this genitive theology.

1.5. This leads to what I see as the most adequate description of feminist theology, namely, as *a critical liberation theology*, not based on the specific nature of women as such, but on the way they historically experience suffering, their psychical and sexual oppression, their infantilisation and their elimination from the structures in the Churches and in society as a result of the prevailing sexism.[6]

This theology examines among other topics the crisis situation of women in the Church and sees there one of the causes of the crisis through which the Church itself is passing. By carefully analysing the situation from the angle of a rebellious but constructive praxis, inspired by a sisterhood seen as a beneficial *communio*, and by striving for a more spontaneous and bodily liturgy as well as a more 'whole-some' theology, the feminist theology seeks to contribute to the good and the wholeness of all those who feel repressed and to the transformation of the Church's structures and male dominance.

The critical function of this theology clearly includes the way in which scripture, tradition and history are interpreted.

Finally, feminists should not overlook that this critical function implies self-criticism. The decision to achieve greater personal wholeness, to inspire men to look at themselves and to put aside their age-old dominance, and to convert a whole Church, all this demands primarily of feminists that they have the courage to be God's partners, called to rise above themselves; the courage not to slip back into that 'turning in on themselves', a situation imposed upon women because they feel they are not left any choice; the courage to say 'yes' to the radical message of love of Christ's gospel, and to say 'no' to the 'temptation' to be accommodating, to get themselves tied to a compromise and so to be deprived of their own strength; in short, the courage to be 'awkward' and annoy the male establishment.[7]

In its reflection on the faith feminist theology covers all those who are unfree and have been turned into mere 'objects', but it remains aware of the fact that in the end women are practically always and everywhere the most oppressed among the oppressed. This means that it is the male (usually their husbands) who lay down who they are, how they differ from them, and, above all, how they are treated as a 'sex'.

2. SOME CHARACTERISTIC FEATURES OF FEMINIST THEOLOGY

2.1. *Formally and methodologically*

First of all, it assumes a broadening of the concept of theology. In feminist theology, theology is understood as reflecting upon a praxis which already exists and is an element of this theology; also, as the reflection on experiences actually spelt out and on the analysis of current unjust and, in the present context, sexist structures. These aspects are, of course, distinct, but, as in other liberation theologies, they should not be separated: action and reflection belong together. In theology analysing the praxis only makes sense if it leads to critical questions, re-formulations, and the liberation and enrichment of theology itself.

Thus feminist theology provides an analytical way of arriving at a better understanding of what happened in the course of history and a strategy to achieve a deeper and broader concept of what the Church is, the ecclesiastical office, charism and prophecy.[8] Here one has at least to mention, without in any way doing justice to the point, the connection between feminism and socialism. The point is that we have to analyse why and how patriarchy and capitalism are so closely intertwined and re-inforce each other. This will lead to the conclusion that feminism, as opposed to patriarchy, and socialism, as opposed to capitalism, need each other if we ever want to bring about a new and truly human freedom for all. Feminism runs the risk of remaining suspended in high ideals and noble motivations, of becoming abstract and losing touch with reality, if it neglects the economic factors which are specific, precise and the product of actual historical development.

On the other hand, socialism needs feminism to get rid of its sexism, understand the damage it has already done, and to respect the value of the human person as such and inter-personal relations. Feminist theology is therefore committed to factual analysis and an inspiration based on faith[9]—and who can deny the importance of this?

In this way feminist theology may well become a vital way of breaking down barriers which obstruct life at large and have driven away countless disheartened women from Church and religion. By the same token it will keep the fire of the religious dimension burning in feminism as such. Feminist theology is a 'holistic' theology. It aims at doing away with the whole wretched separation of body and spirit, man and woman, man and God, East and West, nature and history. This is not a matter of levelling down but of holding together whatever belongs together in creativity and fruitfulness in a unity which thrives on the tensions between polarities. The total *separation* of these opposites in fact always results in polar-isation, in breaking things apart, and it can only be kept alive by putting one above the other.[10]

This feminist theology is born of a certain 'women-togetherness'. It needs this because then woman can ask their own questions about the ultimate values and can together look for the answers. This exchange, this mutual recognition, this affirmation and understanding confrontation, this search for new images, new formulations and expressions will obviously lead to important creativity. The sense of powerlessness drains away to make room for the experience of a kind of new birth, of really 'being', and of becoming fully and truly 'human'. The fire of the Spirit sparks from one to the other, creates warmth and light between them and within each of them, and so creates a sisterhood. Spirit and Church acquire here a reality, unheard of, un-thought of, and actually moving.

Feminist theology is a process theology, as is borne out by all the studies produced in this field. 'This book is about change and movement; it is about a process and *is* itself a process.'[11] The fact that women have become aware of having been kept down for centuries on end, whether this was justified on the basis 'natural' or 'divine' law or by some theological argument, has made them more open and ready for the unfolding of God's revelation in time and history.

Other epithets could be applied to feminist theology, such as 'inductive', 'pneumatological', 'Utopian-prophetical' and even 'Dionysian'.[12] There is no room for all this. Yet, one point has still to be stressed: feminist theology cannot do without an effective use of what has so far been achieved by those sciences which deal with religion.

Process-philosophy and -theology are not often mentioned explicitly (Mary Daly does so in her *Beyond God the Father*). I have mentioned it myself here because this allows me to introduce some topics which are inherent in feminist theology.

2.2. *The Content of Feminist Theology*

Some authors who have written about process-theology[13] several times mention feminist criticism. They then refer specifically to three levels where process-theology can contribute to the issue of women's liberation. These levels cover (1) ideas and concepts; (2) the use of images and imagery; (3) the use of language. I want to apply this process to the question of 'God'.

2.2.1. (*a*) The concept of God

Feminist theology, like process theology, objects to a God who is exclusively self-sufficient, omniscient and all-powerful, the Totally Other, an immutable and exclusively transcendental God (typically characterised by features that stress 'power'), a God for whom we are but insignificant little creatures. We rather stress the God who turns to us as a partner in love, who is gentle, vulnerable and near—'God as creative and responsive love'.[14]

(*b*) The image of God

By now it is well known that feminist theology rejects a male and patriarchal God. These were not the terms in which God revealed himself to Israel. On the contrary, he expressed himself in a refreshingly unfanciful way: JHWH—He who is, He who will be with us, He who causes existence, who is the source and ground of being, and who deploys himself in being.

Apart from the male and patriarchal features in which the faithful have dressed up this God, Scripture also provides, though less frequently, maternal images which, however, played no important part in practice or in the way theologians operated in history. One can trace these fluctuations through the centuries in the images which were meant to symbolise God's nearness. In the Roman Catholic Church Mary assumes prominence as the emphasis falls more on the divine nature of Christ. In the Reformation Jesus himself is occasionally endowed with 'feminine' features, as in the devotional literature of pietism.

Today there are those who want to restore the balance by stressing human aspects which are just as capable of 'imaging' the divine as others, amusingly expressed in the fictitious reply of the astronauts to the Russians' question: 'Did you see God?' The answer was: 'Yes, and she's black'. Others, like Whitehead, prefer the use of images broad enough to imply what are supposed to be 'feminine' features: God as infinitely patient, tender, and wise.

(c) The matter of language

Language is a process, and a complex one. It gives expression to common images, and so influences our own way of looking at things. But this is a chicken-and-egg process because language itself is moulded by what we need to express in images. New images and symbols are not imposed by decree but emerge from the deeper layers of our consciousness which open the way for new and original images, simply through a more cautious, a more carefully descriptive and more pointed use of language.

Summing up

God is not static, but dynamic. God is an operational term, not a self-sufficient naming word (Daly). He is a source of disturbing but creative chaos in so far as this leads to a transformation of the existing present. If this 'present' covers only one half of reality, is cut down, and cries out for 'wholeness'; if it is rigid and calls out for renewal; if it is a dormant potential, waiting to be roused and brought to actuality, then, obviously, such a transformation becomes imperative. This means that here God's immanence becomes more immediately relevant than his transcendence—at least if we truly believe that our existence is a participation in his existence in a reciprocity both offered and accepted.

2.2.2. *Christology*

The prophetic quality of the way in which Jesus mixed with all the 'fringe' people—and this included women—indicates and reveals the loving way in which God concerns himself with all people and helps up those that are trampled underfoot. But feminist theology gets into deeper waters when it objects to the dogma that with the life, death and resurrection God's revelation not only became definitive but was actually closed. This would mean that theology has nothing else to do but to see what it can get out of the coffer of the *depositum fidei*. This then makes it easy to insist on the power-structures which happened to develop in history and which happen to exclude all women from any responsibility and mediation in the spreading of salvation with—of all arguments—the naïve assertion that Jesus was male.

For this reason feminist theology prefers the inductive to the deductive approach. It believes in an on-going incarnation which manifests itself in the new birth of all those who are oppressed and of all the women who only now are beginning to exist in their own right, to speak for themselves, to be recognised as full persons and to express the faith as they see it. God continues to become human. Jesus Christ demonstrated and lived out God's voidance of power by replacing it with service.

2.2.3. *Pneumatology*

In 1975 I was allowed to introduce feminist theology in Holland.[15] At the time it was rather rough and ready and very indebted to American publications. But already I was worried about the absence of pneumatology, and yet I feel that here we have a valuable springboard for the further growth of feminist theology.

We know that in early Semitic language the word for 'spirit' was the feminine '*ruach*'. Later on, the west either used the Greek word *pneuma* which is neutral, or the Latin word *spiritus* which is masculine. And so it came about that in the west the concept of the Trinity could be conveniently expressed in terms which had a masculine bias to them. And so the *ruach*-Jahweh came to yield to the *Logos* in the gospel of St John, which represented the separating, creative, powerful 'Word' of which the distinct clarity differed from the fluent and ambiguous image of the brooding dove—symbol of warmth and fertility.

I hope I have made it clear that, in so far as I am concerned, feminist theology is pre-eminently pneumatological and tries to draw attention to the flexibility with which God operates in the Spirit.

In theology three areas correspond to the three ways in which God reveals himself: the theology of creation, Christology and pneumatology, and of these three pneumatology has clearly been underrated. We simply have to establish a mutually inspiring interaction between these three kinds of revelation. This would bring out the way in which God communicates and would strike the balance between transcendence and immanence. Only in this communicative aspect of the trinity can Christian *anthropology* acquire the significance it deserves.[16]

2.2.4. *Anthropology*

To put it in still another way: Scripture offers us a whole range of images and structures which express relationship, e.g., God-people, God-Sophia (Wisdom), Christ-Church, etc. All these expressions show God 'in a wealth of relationships which take shape as history, as encounter and as process'. The same wealth of relationship is embodied in the teaching of the Trinity. If man, then, was created in the image of God, it means that man, too, must be a converging of relationships, and must be understood as such: in her/his existence, in the history and the structures of partnership.[17]

I want to stress that 'partnership' here means for me the whole range of the relations and structures which denote reciprocity among people individually, between the sexes, between people and nature/cosmos, and, as the foundation of it all, between mankind and God. This does not mean the kind of relationship which subordinates one to another, nor that of 'complementarity' which makes each cling to his/her own unchangeable nature and the accepted pecking-order but will allow for some contribution by the other. What is meant here is a diversity of relationships which, however different, is about giving and taking, about mutual enrichment and the wholeness of each person.

2.2.5. *Ethical aspects*

Sexism is both an anthropological, psychological sin and a structural evil. There must be conversion at both levels. We have to reject the patriarchal attitude—the 'strong' man imposing his will on others and considering them his property. We have to eliminate androcentrism—as long as man occupies the cultural and political centre of our society women will obviously float on the periphery. We have to abandon that kind of masculine dualism which does not merely turn woman into something 'other' but degrades her by projecting on to her all those features which man is scared of developing in himself, which he therefore considers of only secondary importance and then attributes—to women. This degradation of woman, as in the whole matter of the male sex trying to define the female sex, is really objectifying the female sex, turning woman into an object, and this prevents any genuine reciprocity between man and woman. In her excellent article on 'The personalisation of human sexuality' Rosemary Ruether has described how liberation should proceed if women are ever to become free of male dominance and achieve true reciprocity.[18]

There is no solution to be found in so-called sexual liberation, nor in the hypocrisy of double standards in morality. Novels and poetry clearly show that women are looking for an unpossessive, playful eroticism which does not necessarily have to end up with an orgasm as the only product; for a simple and cheerful reciprocity without 'that damned genital seriousness which I have never understood'.[19]

Feminist theology is therefore a liberation theology. Whatever the differences in cultural, psychological, social and political circumstances, it seeks to promote the abolition of the wretched separation, polarisation and mutual degradation of the two sexes. This must be done by releasing the 'feminine' principle in men so that they, too, become 'whole' persons; by allowing full scope to both the 'feminine' and the 'masculine' principle in women, in other words, by giving women the chance to become full persons who establish their own identity; by humanising the structures and stripping them of their harsh, male, competitive aspects (I have in mind here, among other things, economy, ecology, technology, war and peace);[20] by overcoming the stereotyped use of 'male' and 'female' and lifting it all to the level of the rich diversity of the fully 'human'.

3. DEALING WITH SCRIPTURE[21]

Since feminism is the expression of a radical change in the way women live their existential, spiritual and bodily life, it is bound to raise many and wide-ranging questions of interpretation. The spiral process of hermeneutics has its roots in the historicity of human existence and hence also of all human understanding. This understanding implies that the way one understands onself, i.e., one's own existence plays an interpretative and critical part in this understanding.

The point therefore is that feminist theology has to deal with scriptural texts in a way which is open-minded, critical and challenging (and in this order!). It is therefore entitled to distinguish between texts which are patriarchal and conditioned by culture and see women as a non-person, and those which show God's liberating intervention breaking through, including that in favour of the humanisation of women.

However, the preoccupation with prior self-understanding, and the interpretation and criticism of the Church order, faith and theology that prevails at present might lead us into two snares which we must avoid.

First, we should not *underrate* the situation in scripture. Our self-understanding could turn into a prejudice, a *parti-pris*, if we assume that a general context conditioned by a patriarchal culture leaves no room whatever for a personalist liberation message for women in divine revelation.

Secondly, we should not *overrate* the situation either. The wish to find in scripture something which will inspire and identify 'women-in-protest' might lead feminist theologians to 'read into' Scripture things which are not there. They might not accept the fact that, realistically speaking, the scriptural context is rather limited; that the profile of women and the words attributed to them were thought up by men who could not possibly have a clue about what is going on today, namely, that women are protesting because they want to be full human persons, 'subjects' instead of 'objects', not tied down to their bodily condition and their potential maternity.

Every theology, feminist or not, implies the search for an answer based on faith. Scripture and tradition can open up and point to a new creative development within the faith in a basically new situation.[22] The scriptural scholar Trible says the same thing in other words: Contexts can change texts and prevent them from becoming petrified.[23] Women should take their cue from God's covenant with humanity, his people, and from his liberating and loving dealings with human beings in a game of love, in the way Jesus exploded taboos in his contact with women. Feminist theology will have to concentrate on the experience of women of today and the way they live, and be able to distinguish between what is universal and what is incidental in the present stage of salvation history.

4. DIALOGUE

In conclusion there is this point: just as the feminists need their own time and place to explain things to each other, to shape their experiences and thoughts, to articulate their hopes and expectations adequately and intelligibly, to develop their plans and strategies, and to celebrate in a new way their relation to God, to each other and to the world at large, so, it seems to me, there seems to develop the need for a dialogue with other liberation theologies and with theologians for whom the understanding of the faith lies in the world-situation and the actual condition of the Churches. Theology becomes a dialogue.

If we want to make this dialogue fruitful for all the participants, two things seem to me to be indispensable.

4.1. The first is an attitude of openness, of being ready to listen with real interest, to put one's own theological 'position' aside, to be receptive and able to reason things out with others, and, for the moment, not to force arguments to prove oneself right and in any case not to prejudge the other side. Without these conditions it would be better not to start a dialogue as yet: in such a case one is only fit for a sharp-edged debate where every position is spelt out in detail. Dialogue is something different: there the partners aim at mutual enrichment through mutual understanding. It is not about 'victory' or 'defeat' but about changing people.[24]

4.2. This condition is not only necessary in order to start with the right attitude but also for the content of the dialogue. The reason is that the dialogue feminist theology is looking for contains the 'strange', the 'unusual' or 'unaccustomed' as an inherent part of its content as well as a principle of theological interpretation which can open up new avenues of human experience. If we want to penetrate reality, the hermeneutic principle is not what is obvious, but what is strange and surprising.[25]

In our case, this open-ended character of the dialogue is necessary, above all, for the dialogue between feminist theologians themselves, who all have their own outlook, as in the case of Daly, Ruether, Russell (all three have published new studies in 1979).[26] It is still more important for the dialogue which is developing between feminist theology in Latin America and 'Black' theology on the one hand, and us, Western feminist theologians, on the other. Yet, I keep on hoping that male theologians will turn up who are prepared to *listen*—surely, every country must have a few of them?[27]

This last point is mentioned, not primarily because, like all theologies, feminist theology must be prepared to submit to the process of verification and falsification, but rather because it has to broaden its potential for development and to make this development work on male theology in the hope that it will shed the over-confidence acquired by a 2000 years' long monologue.

It just may happen that we then shall move together in a direction where we understand each other and in this way serve the cause of reconciliation, liberation and peace in our own way

Translated by T. L. Westow

Notes

1. There is a vast but diverse bibliography. Yet, this theology is barely ten years old and still seeking its way. So I am limited to merely introducing a feminist theology which is still growing, pointing out some basic factors, mentioning some problems, and so inviting the reader to read for her/himself. An extensive bibliography may be obtained from 'Feminisme en Christendom' at the theological

Faculty of the Catholic University of Nijmegen, Heyendaalseweg 121A, Nijmegen, Holland.

2. Kari Elisabeth Børresen 'Antropogische fundamenten van man-vrouw-verhouding in de klassieke theologie' *Concilium* 12 (1976) 18-30.

3. Dagny Kaul 'Principal lines in feminist theology' *The Bible and Our Future* (preparatory guidelines for the W.S.C.F. Conference, to take place in Norway, August 1979).

4. Mary Condren 'For the banished children of Eve: an introduction to feminist theology' *Movement* (SCM) 24 (no year) 21-23.

5. See, e.g., Letty Russell *Human Liberation in a Feminist Perspective—A Theology* (Philadelphia 1974) pp. 52-53; Kurt Lüthi *Gottes neue Eva* (Stuttgart/Berlin 1978) pp. 50-52.

6. Elisabeth Schüssler Fiorenza 'Feminist theology as a critical theology of liberation' *Theological Studies* 36 (1975) 605-626; the same author also addressed the Women's Ordination Conference in Baltimore, November 1978, but its report has not yet been published. See also Dorothée Sölle 'Remembering Christ: Faith, Theology and Liberation' *Radical Religion* 3 No. 2 (1977) 12-18.

7. See Ino Bieżeno 'Een vrouw die in de weg liep: Catharina van Siëna' *Reliëf* 43 No. 7/8 (1975).

8. See Mary Hunt's address to the Baltimore Women's Ordination Conference (see note 6).

9. Sheila D. Collins 'Socialism and feminism: a necessary ground for liberation' *Cross Currents* 26 (1976) 33-47; *ibid* 'Feminism and Socialism' *Radical Religion* 3 No. 2 (1977) 5-12 (main theme of this issue).

10. Nelle Morton 'Towards a whole theology' *Sexism in the 1970s* (Geneva 1975) pp. 56-65.

11. e.g., Clare Benedicks Fischer, a.o. *Women in a strange land* (Philadelphia 1975) p. 2.

12. Sam Keen 'Manifesto for a Dionysian theology' *Cross Currents* 19 No. 1 (1968-9) 37-55; see A. Burnier *De zwembadmentaliteit* (Amsterdam 1979) 76-97.

13. John B. Cobb Jr. and David Ray Griffin *Process Theology* (Philadelphia 1976) Chapter 3 and pp. 132-135.

14. e.g., Mary Condren—see note 4.

15. Tine (Govaart) Halkes 'Feminist theology versus a patriarchal Religion' *Feminology, Proceedings of the Dutch-Scandinavian symposium on woman's position in society* (Nijmegen 1975) pp. 44-58.

16. Dagny Kaul 'Principal lines in feminist theology' *The Bible and Our Future* pp. 22 f (see note 3); see also Kurt Lüthi *Gottes neue Eva* pp. 197 f (see note 5).

17. Kurt Lüthi *ibid.*; see Elisabeth Moltmann-Wendel 'Partnerschaft. Studie zur Entwicklung des theologischen und kirchlichen Partnerschaftbegriffes seit 1945' in Claudia Pinl a.o. *Frauen auf neuen Wegen* (Gelnhausen/Berlin 1978); Letty Russell *The Future of Partnership* (Philadelphia 1979).

18. Eugene G. Bianchi on Rosemary R. Ruether *From Machismo to Mutuality* (New York 1976) pp. 70-87.

19. Verena Stefan *Ontwenning* n.p. 1975) p. 46.

20. Feminism as a critique of culture and a counter-culture is an indispensable

partner in the dialogue about 'faith, science and the future' if we want to create a viable society, but it is difficult for this idea to penetrate, as was shown even in the W.C.C. Conference on that topic in Boston 1979 (see the Preparatory Readings for that conference: see *Faith, Science and the Future*, Geneva 1978).

21. I deal with this question more extensively in a book that will appear in 1980 (Gütersloh, Germany, and Kampen, Netherlands). See also Maria De Groot a.o. 'Schritte auf dem Wege zur Menschwerdung' in C. Pinl, a.o. *Frauen auf neuen Wegen* (Gelnhausen/Berlin 1978) pp. 201-220, and in Halkes and Buddingh (ed.) *Als vrouwen aan het Woord komen* (2nd ed. 1978) pp. 27-43 and 47-53.

22. E. C. F. A. Schillebeeckx 'Het chirstelijk huwelijk en de menselijke realiteit van volkomen huwelijksontwrichting' in Th. A. G. van Eupen (ed.) *(On)ontbindbaarheid van het huwelijk* 58 (1970) of the Annalen Thijmgenootschap Hilversum pp. 207-208; *ibid. The Understanding of Faith* (London and New York 1974).

23. Phyllis Trible *God and the Rhetoric of Sexuality* (Philadelphia 1978) pp. 3, 4, 202 and *passim*.

24. Kurt Lüthi *Gottes neue Eva* p. 53; Catherina J. M. Halkes *De horizon van het pastorale gesprek* (Haarlem 1977) pp. 15-16.

25. The idea of this category of the 'strange' came to me from H. J. van Hout in his review of H. Friedli's book *Fremdheit als Heimat* (Zürich 1974) in *Saamhorig*, the journal of the Dutch Council of Churches (n. 10, December 1978).

26. See Carter Hayward 'Ruether and Daly: Theologians—Speaking and Sparking, Building and Burning' in *Christianity and Crisis* 39 (2 April 1979) pp. 66-72.

27. To name only two Dutch authors whose work contributed to women's liberation, also from the theological angle, I refer to René van Eyden and Auke Jelsma.

Maria Agudelo

The Church's Contribution
to the
Emancipation of Women

1. INTRODUCTION

ANY ATTEMPT at a synthesis of such a debated subject, particularly
one aimed at readers from such differing cultural backgrounds, seems to
me a highly rash undertaking. The place of women in the Church, as in
society, is continually changing; in the west it is one thing, in the east
another; in Latin America it has some special features; in Africa it
presents very different aspects. Furthermore, I know from my experience
of lectures and seminars that my Latin American viewpoint is liable to
appear timid, excessively moderate and even trivial to women in Europe
and North America.

To define my own position honestly: I do not belong to any organised
feminist movement (nor to any 'anti' group), but I do sympathise with
what has been called 'the second feminism': this does not seek to find a
place for women in a Church (understood in its aspect of a human society)
of men, but to understand and make others understand that the Church
has to be a place for both men and women, and to help this Church to
become one that acts for the good of all, to be an active, conscious and
forceful impetus to a real *conversion*. The Spirit requires an overall and
fundamental conversion, which will be seen in our concern for oppressed
groups. This is what I take Paul VI to have been referring to when he
spoke of 'a deeper objective than ... mere equality of rights ... an
objective which will allow men and women to pool their specific riches

124

and dynamism to build a world no longer stratified but unified'. This task is to be seen as something 'that cannot be achieved through programmes conceived at summits by an élite, for the élite', but which demands 'a maturation and renewal of life at local community level'.[1]

So if I dare to write on the subject, despite my reservations, it is because I believe it important to consider—before it is too late—the theoretical elements that will provide the coordinates of this conversion. Because I would like to contribute my own loyal effort to the common task of building a serving Church, a leaven in the mass, a Church where brotherhood can reign.

Perhaps I should add that I do not use the feminist vocabulary. This is not to underestimate the importance of the structure of language; contact with groups such as 'Femmes et hommes dans l'Eglise' and LCWR have taught me how important it can be. In my native Spanish, for example, there is no word for 'sisterhood' to place alongside 'brotherhood'; in many languages we say 'men' to refer to both sexes: language expresses a whole gamut of collective unconscious attitudes bred in to us by a *machisto* civilisation.

2. AN ATTEMPT AT OBJECTIVITY

We are all becoming used to the fierce criticism of the Church, from inside as well from out, for its attitude to women. It seems to me only fair to point out that when we admit our failings in this respect we should realise that society in general outside the Church is hardly less guilty of the same failings. This is not to excuse us or to bury the problem, but to appreciate its extent. One illustration: in 1975—International Year of Woman—the United Nations, which proclaimed it such, employed some 40,000 people, of which half were women. In the higher echelons of this army of employees, 80 per cent were men; in the lower ranks, 70 per cent were women. At the highest level, there was 1 woman to 34 men; at the second highest, 8 women and 292 men.

But it is equally important to be objective from the other side: although it is true that Christianity treats women as full human beings and that the figure of Mary has given the world the prototype of the free and definitive woman, there is no denying that there are still many grey areas between theory and practice: in theory, even, the Church has failed to take account of the best that the social sciences have said about feminity; in practice, sacralised structures—such as canon law and liturgical norms—have contributed not a little to relegating women to second-class faithful; finally, in most local Church communities, women's role in pastoral work is one of helping rather than really participating.

3. GREY AREAS BETWEEN THEORY AND PRACTICE

Feminism should be a fact for the Church, a sign of the times challenging it by its very presence in the world, although it is not something hatched in its bosom or with its consent. The question for the Church, therefore, is not whether to be 'pro' or 'contra'—particularly since as a recognition of the dignity of the human person and a way to brotherhood feminism has its real roots in Christianity—but rather of knowing how to read this sign in order to fulfil its mission of service to and fomenting of a new humanity. That is to say: faced with the ever-increasing clamour for women to be seen and recognised in a different way, the Church's task is to guide this dynamism towards a new man-woman relationship and therefore towards a new society and a new Church.

The official Church has understood this and stated as much. *Gaudium et Spes* gave us women real hope when it proclaimed: 'Any form of discrimination in the field of human rights . . . based on sex . . . should be superseded and eliminated as contrary to God's plan' (n. 29). We might ask: has this text been given juridical status? As far as application goes, has it ever been more than a pious hope?

There is an interesting passage from the 1971 Synod of Bishops—particularly if one knows its genesis: 'We stress that women should have their own part of responsibility and participation in the communitary life of society and also of the Church.'[2] In the first draft text voted on, this passage read: '. . . that women should have a share of responsibility and a participation *equal to that of men* in social life and in the Church'. Such a statement would have had such far-reaching consequences that it would have been Utopic to imagine it getting through, which it did not. This is not to say that the Synod overthrew the teaching of *Gaudium et Spes*, but rather that it drew back from drawing all the consequences for the life of the Church from the principle it laid down. This is why it suggested the subject might be studied in greater depth, through a Commission. And the Pontifical Commission on the rights of women in society and in the Church was indeed set up.

But the text in its final form is interesting enough: 'We stress that women should have *their own part* of responsibility and participation. . . .' The passage comes in the chapter on 'The Achievement of Justice', in the section dealing with 'The Witness of the Church', in which is stated: 'If the Church wishes to witness to justice, it recognises that those who speak of justice should themselves appear just in the eyes of men.' Therefore, if it claims to recognise the rights and responsibilities of women in the Church, it should make a sincere effort to bring justice and right about within itself. Hence the basic principle of justice: each to his own, and therefore to women, *their own part* of responsibility and participation. With which, it seems to me, we are back in the old trap of reserving specific roles to women which end up by denying basic equality. When 'differences' become so 'specific', they justify discrimination. So women have their own part as women and not an equal part with men.

4. INCORPORATING VALID OBSERVATIONS FROM THE SOCIAL SCIENCES

This leads on to the subject of what is specific to feminity considered in relation to changing historical and cultural data. This is a fascinating subject, but one dealt with by other articles in this issue. What would obviously please everyone would be for the Church to take account of valid scientific observations in its official pronouncements on the subject, and, furthermore, to draw the logical consequences from these observations. This is plainly not easy, since the social sciences are far from having clarified every aspect of the subject, and discussions are often tinged with ideological prejudices. There is still a long way to go before we have an adequate theology of sexuality, the theme of vocation needs deeper examination, and there is a dearth of women theologians to contribute to the debates.

Another aspect is that a centuries-old tradition of pious writing on the Virgin Mary has sacralised passivity and remaining in the background. This has helped to keep women out of positions of responsible participation in affairs, and reinforced the image of women as delicate and weak, whose vocation in life is humble and dependent service. The more she humbles herself for the benefit of the male, the more feminine she is.

The Church does sometimes manage to escape from this scheme of things in its official capacity, which cannot fail to be beneficial on every level, particularly that of pastoral care. So Paul VI, in presenting the Virgin Mary as an inspiration to modern woman, was able to speak of woman today as 'desirous of participating with decision-making powers in the affairs of the community', and therefore viewing with joy the Virgin who gave her active and responsible consent 'not to the solution of a temporary problem, but to the work of centuries . . . the Incarnation'.

But how can we present Mary as an example of woman participating decisively in the history of humanity and not give the same role to woman today?

5. STRUCTURES

There is one general complaint that we can make most insistently against the Church: why, while in the rest of the world legislation advancing women's rights has been making headway for a century, has canon law remained basically unchanged for decades, and, that it is being revised, why is this being done without any participation by women, either on the Commission or among the advisers? Liturgical rules, the rest of written legislation and internal organisation of the Church are still, it seems to me, operating on a level that hovers between timidity, concessions and ignorance of the situation. One thing must be absolutely clear to everyone: the Church cannot go on evading the feminist challenge, which is not confined to asking for women to be ordained. It is not a matter of trying to obtain certain concessions, not even this one which has come to be seen, even by those not fighting for it, as the 'Gordian knot' of institutional resistance. Situations are not changed by decrees, but by something quite different, something that commits both men and women, that has to be sought by both of them together in an investigation into reality, in thought and in prayer, in an attempt, for example, to draw out the full meaning of the phrase 'In Christ there is neither male nor female' (Gal. 3:28). Recognising that women are theoretically equal before God does not produce recognition of their equality in the daily life of humanity. This will need—and needs—a long, long struggle, and ascesis: if there are to be real changes on the level of structures and actual situations, there must be deep changes on the level of images and mentality.

6. PARTICIPATING IN PASTORAL WORK

The basic aspect of the Church's effort in relation to women must be for them to move from influence to responsibility.

In society as a whole, we cannot go on confusing feminism with an appearance of liberation, with the compensatory reaction that makes women compare themselves to men and try to be their equals, instead of accepting themselves as different, as though this meant recognising themselves as inferior. Work is an important element in this process. Work needs to be conceived away from the framework of the falsely idealised 'little woman', fit only for embroidery and cooking. It needs to be seen in terms of raising children, of transforming the world, and of personal fulfilment. This viewpoint must be applied to professional work as well as to the redistribution of domestic and educational tasks with its repercussions on the organisation of family life and society in general.

The same applies to the mission of the Church: we want to be a presence where the meaning and credibility of the man-woman relationship, and its service to humanity, are decided. Once again, this is not a question of legislation and decrees; no decision handed down by authority, but the patient and concerted effort of the whole people of God—including authority—will bring this about. . . . But how much longer, we must ask, will the authority be composed of men only?

There are many women in the Church suffering the frustrating experience of something that might be called either 'irresponsible authority' or 'responsibility without authority'. Sooner or later we must reach the stage of having responsible authority, collegially expressed, in the service of the mission of the Church, which will enable men and women to find a way of 'doing truth in charity'—together.

The women religious of Brazil met in Petropolis in 1974 to discuss nuns' participation in the International Year of Woman, and insisted on the need for women to be given real responsibility, and the right to education for it, in the belief that bishops and priests would understand what we were talking about. Such an understanding has, however, not become widespread. More common is the following type of conversation, between a man in a position of authority in the Church and a woman who wants to participate in the work of the Church. It usually ends in mutual misunderstanding, and runs something like this. He asks: 'But what do you women really want? Aren't you already taking an active part in the liturgy, acting as members of pastoral teams, parish and even diocesan councils? Some of you have even been appointed university chaplains; you are the driving force behind all sorts of social services; you run retreat houses, you are missionaries in a way that used to be reserved for men.' To which she replies: 'Yes, but . . . we are not involved in pastoral work on the level at which strategic decisions are taken, the decisions that might change our whole way of acting and point the Church in completely new basic directions. We can be appointed to all sorts of posts without feeling really responsible.'

Underlying this approach there is not so much proud independence nor a challenge born of frustration, but a sincere wish for a Vatican II-style Church, a Church of presence and service, in which the mainspring is not an authority imposing views, organising, finding subordinates to help it, but a common activity by men and women seeking a better humanity to receive and bring about salvation.

There are no small difficulties in the way of bringing this state of affairs about. If women are to have 'a share of responsibility and a participation equal to that of men in social life and in the Church', we need objective, de-ideologised evidence that they are capable of sustaining such a share. Specific information is much better than theory here; it is more important to show that women have carried out particular roles well in various areas of the Church's life than to spend time theorising over whether they are capable of doing so.

Education, at least in some parts of the world, is also a major problem. In many countries women's educational opportunities are still inferior to men's; the underdeveloped countries generally show a discriminatory pattern within the general oppression they suffer from, falling harder on women than on men. Women need the opportunity for higher education, particularly in theology, if they are to discourse on equal terms with bishops and priests formed by years of seminary and university education. Nuns have generally been in the best position to obtain this, and this is why, of all women in the Church, they have been foremost in looking for and developing new forms of ministry and service, new forms of authority and responsibility, and new forms of spirituality related to poverty and people's aspirations to liberation and social justice.

7. MINISTRIES

This leads to the question of ministries. If we accept an ecclesiology that sees the whole Church as ministerial, with a great diversity of diaconates inspired by the Spirit, then ministries outside those of the bishop and presbyter should no longer be regarded as subordinate or secondary to the one priestly (hierarchical) ministry, but as each indispensable in its way, something brought into being by the Spirit, with its own dignity and meaning, something that the hierarchy of the Church should coordinate and value for the common good of all.

If this is so, then ministries open to women should not be lacking in real responsibility and decision-making, otherwise their position of inferiority to men, of helpmate and handmaid, will be maintained. I am not talking of the creation of 'women's ministries', because the creation of such a category could easily lead to discrimination or reinforce it.

Women's role in the Church lies within the sphere of the laity. Without denying the progress that has been made, there is no escaping the fact that one of the Church's social sins is an excess of clericalism. This is an historical fact, but another is that the new Church among us (in Latin America, that is), under the impetus of the Basic Ecclesial Communities, is producing real and effective participation by lay people, men and women, in the promotion of the saving mission of the Church, which is its service in the world. This has not come about by episcopal decree (though in many of our churches the understanding attitude of bishops with real pastoral experience has been a major factor, as we saw at Puebla), but in the same way that most basic human progress has been made, by common consent and action.

The tradition of the Church is invaluable in this process, but provided we go back to the tradition of a Church not identified with the hierarchy—though respecting it as such—a Church not prepared with a ready answer to every question, but asking the questions, a non-clericalised Church, the people of God. In this Church which the Spirit is making spring from the people, a determined feminism is not only accepted but deepened in its main thrust: acceptance and mutual recognition of men and women working together for the Kingdom.

This view of an all-ministerial Church is one of the reasons why we in

Latin America are not fighting directly at present for the priestly ordination of women: we are afraid it might lead to a strengthening of clerical power. This is not to say we do not regard the question as important; it is in fact the touchstone of attitudes to women and to the man-woman relationship. What we can perhaps say is that when we achieve a deeper and more serene view of sexuality, the dignity of women in ritual and ministry will be fully recognised.

Women in Latin America have followed the debates on the subject with interest, been concerned over its setbacks, accepted the papal pronouncements on the subject with respect, but without becoming passionate over this aspect of the matter. We do not believe history moves forward in jumps, and do not see women priests as the final, absolute and ultimate goal, nor even the next one. For us, as in some of the Protestant Churches, the real responsibility will probably continue in male hands. The overall framework of our culture means there is still a long way to travel, on the roads of theory, psychology, culture and practice. If we look at the most basic aspects of our psychology and culture, the prejudices become more difficult to overcome the more irrational they are. Also, we fear that women, if they copy existing patterns, will become involved in bureaucracy, identified with the pyramidal structure of ecclesiastical organisation which encourages clericalism. We feel that among the poor, power will alienate us from the people, just when in Latin America the Spirit is fomenting and consolidating a model of the Church which springs from the people. Something of the sort happens when women are admitted to diocesan councils, when they take part in National Assemblies of bishops, when places are found for them in the Curia. There are no real obstacles to their being there: there are women capable of these tasks, and the tasks themselves are important. But perhaps this is not the best way: it could be just bolstering up an ecclesiastical structure whose continuance in its present form is not in fact desirable.

The Latin American Church, that of the Medellín and Puebla, the Church that has opted in favour of the poor and of justice, has not made the emancipation of women a special issue. Nor has the theology of liberation. Yet it would be unfair to suggest that our more progressive bishops and our theologians are dismissive or unconcerned on this question. The situation is rather that when one links evangelisation to overall liberation and fights as a Church for a redeemed brotherhood of a society, the emancipation of women has a natural place in the wider struggle.

8. CONCLUSION

Whatever stage we have reached in our respective local churches, one fact is indisputable: the call for the emancipation of women is a sign of the times, a challenge and a responsibility. It challenges men and women, the hierarchy and the faithful, the clergy as much as the laity; we all have to be evangelists, and this means a Church in which no-one is used, but in which we are all partners in its mission.

Translated by Paul Burns

Notes

1. *Osservatore Romano* 19 (April 1975).
2. *Justice in the World* III 40 n. 42.

Contributors

MANUEL ALCALÁ, S.J., was born in Granada in 1926, became a Jesuit in 1943 and was ordained priest in 1957. He gained a licentiate in journalism in the Escuela Oficial de Madrid with a dissertation on *Luis Bunuel: Cine e ideologia* (Madrid 1973). He was university chaplain in Seville until 1968. Since then he has worked in the Casa de Escritores and the Jesuit 'Centro Loyola' in Madrid where he is editorial adviser to the journals *Razon y Fe* and *Resena*. During the last ten years he has been visiting professor in the theological faculties of Granada and Madrid-Comillas Universities. The subject of women and ministries is one of his many interests and this resulted in the publication of *Lamujer y los ministerios en la Iglesia* (Madrid 1979), which he intends to amplify.

MARGARET BRENNAN, I.H.M., is associate professor of pastoral theology at Regis College of the Toronto School of Theology and staff member of the Spiritual Integration Programme. She has published and lectured widely on the subject of women in ministry.

ELIZABETH CARROLL, R.S.M., is vice-president of the Pittsburgh Sisters of Mercy. After her doctorate in Mediaeval History, Sister Elizabeth had served as faculty member and administrator of Mount Mercy/Carlow College 1945-1966. Following her term as President of the Pittsburgh Sisters of Mercy 1964-1974 she served as Staff Associate of the Center of Concern in Washington D.C. from 1974-1978, where she directed the project of Women in Church and Society. In that capacity she keynoted the First Women's Ordination Conference in Detroit, 1975, and spoke at the second in Baltimore, 1978. She is a member of the Core Commission of Women's Ordination Conference. Her writings include *Experience of Women Religious in the Ministry of the Church* (Illinois 1973); 'The "Proper Place" for Women in the Church' in

Women and Catholic Priesthood ed. A. M. Gardiner (New York 1976); 'Women in the Life of the Church' in *Women Priests: A Catholic Commentary on the Vatican Declaration* ed. Leonard Swidler and Arlene Swidler (New York 1977).

M. NADINE FOLEY, O.P., Ph.D., is currently a member of the General Council of the Adrian Dominican Congregation. She has taught philosophy and theology at Barry College, Siena Heights College and Drake University. A pioneer among Roman Catholic women in campus ministry, she held positions in that capacity at the University of New Mexico, University of Houston and Drake. She was the coordinator of the task force which organised the conference Women in Future Priesthood Now—A Call for Action held in Detroit in November, 1975. She currently serves on the Ecclesial Role of Women Committee of the Leadership Conference of Women Religious, the sub-committee on sexist language of the International Commission on English in the Liturgy, and the Board of Directors of the National Liturgical Conference. During the spring semester of 1979, was visiting professor of Ecumenical Relations at the Harvard Divinity School, Cambridge, Massachusetts. She has contributed articles to many journals and symposia mostly on the role of women.

CATHERINA J. M. HALKES lectures at the theological faculty of the Catholic University of Nijmegen, The Netherlands, with the special commission to study and teach the subject of *Feminism and Christendom*.

ROSEMARY HAUGHTON was born in 1924 half American, half English-Jewish. She had a random education, with no degrees (but was granted two honorary degrees later). She married Algernon Haughton in 1948, has seven sons and three daughters, several foster children. Her writing career developed gradually, as did also lecturing in North America in theology and related areas. In 1973 the family became part of a small new community on the land, engaged in therapy for troubled and sick people, also a centre for young people looking for alternatives to 'cosumerism'. Her own work has become increasingly concerned with spiritual guidance, especially of groups seeking their identity as the Church in a new way. This special mission is now a full-time vocation, as family and community find their own way forward. Her best known book is *The Transformation of Man*, and she has written about thirty other books. The most recent, a whole theology, is her major work (to be published in 1980) and will be her last, as her new work is to 'preach the Gospel'. The title of this book is *The Passionate God*.

RENÉ LAURENTIN was born in 1917 in Tours and ordained in 1946. He is professor of theology at the Université de l'Ouest (Angers). He has taught widely at universities in Canada, U.S.A., Italy and Latin America. He was a consultant to the Preparatory Theological Commission for Vatican II and an official expert at the Council. He is a member of the Mariological Academy of Rome and vice-president of the Société française d'études mariales. He is a contributor to *Le Figaro* and writes the column devoted to the Virgin Mary in *La Revue des sciences philosophiques et théologiques*, and exercises a pastoral ministry in the Paris region. His numerous publications deal mainly with the Virgin Mary, Vatican II and the Synods.

FERDINAND MENNE was born in 1941. Since 1978 he has been professor of social education at the Dortmund section of the Ruhr college of education. Among his published works are *Kirchliche Sexualethik gegen gesellschaftliche Realität* (Munich-Mainz 1971) and collaborative volumes and articles on religious groups, alternative life-forms, and personal awareness in modern society.

MARIE DE MERODE DE CROY was born in Rumillies (Belgium) in 1946. She received her higher philosophical and theological education in her native country at the Catholic University of Louvain and now teaches at Princeton Theological Seminary and at the Catechetical Institute at Yonkers. She has published a series of articles on women in the Bible. She is married and has two children.

MARIE AUGUSTA NEAL, S.N.D., is professor of sociology at Emmanuel College in Boston. She was a visiting professor of Sociology at the University of California at Berkeley in 1969 and at Harvard Divinity School from 1973-1975. Her two published books are *Values and Interests in Social Change* (1965) and *A Sociotheology of Letting Go* (1977). Her main research is an extended study of the changing structures of religious congregations of Catholic Women in the United States. She has had a Ford Foundation Grant to study women's roles in society, and has done a study of religious education in Southern Africa. She is currently on the council of the SSSR and is past president of the Association for the Sociology of Religion.

IDA RAMING studied theology and German at Münster and Freiburg, and holds a doctorate in theology from the University of Münster. Her doctoral thesis appeared in English under the title: *The Exclusion of Women from the Priesthood: Divine Law or Sex Discrimination?* (Metuchen, N.J., 1976), and she has written other articles on the position of women in the Church, including one for *Concilium*.